Wasted Tax Dollars For Wasted Time Served... California's Great Prison Travesty and Missed Opportunity

By

Daniel A. O'Farrell

Contributor: Charles Bonner

authorHOUSE

1663 LIBERTY DRIVE, SUITE 200
BLOOMINGTON, INDIANA 47403
(800) 839-8640
www.authorhouse.com

First published by AuthorHouse 11/12/04

ISBN: 1-4184-8243-9 (e)
ISBN: 1-4184-8242-0 (sc)

Library of Congress Control Number: 2004095149

Printed in the United States of America
Bloomington, Indiana

This book is printed on acid-free paper.

Table of Contents

Introduction

Incarceration without education is just doing time.

The minimum prison sentence is usually one to three years. Parole, following prison is another one to three years. This is a lot of mandated, judge-imposed time to get someone's attention. Breaking rocks and boulders or napping on one's bunk bed is not the solution. Teaching someone vocational skills, helping the offender to obtain a GED, if he/she has not completed high school, addressing serious problems with alcohol and drug addiction problems…is. A clean and sober lifestyle, coupled with credentials to gain legal employment, literally changes people lives.

Every state in America has a Department of Corrections. The Departments play an important role in protecting the public by locking up criminal offenders in secure, safe and disciplined institutional settings. Work, academic education, vocational training and some specialized substance abuse treatment are available in few, but not all of the nation's prisons. In most cases, when it is provided, it is far too short in curriculum and lacking in proper facilitating by teachers and counselors.

Most prison programs have been successful in other prisons in the past. They usually provide an attempt at introducing the inmate to the Twelve Steps and other successful AA and NA basic self-help disciplines. These services are usually minimal and not readily accessible to all inmates due to facilitation restraints and constrained budgets.

The chief priority at any prison is security. The largest group of personnel are Corrections Officers. This is understandable, but it is also unbalanced. It creates a powerful resource and opportunity bridled to mediocre work and diminished advantage for the low-skilled and under-schooled inmate population.

The prison scenario described is all too pervasive and typical in today's prison. This book attempts to describe and help fix what can only be described as a great travesty and missed opportunity.

Chapter 1

America's Drug Culture: A Path To Prison

As inmates regain a clean and sober lifestyle in prison, many of them regain a desire to change. The Higher Power spiritualism offered in AA, NA and CA is a priceless commodity that is extremely popular and successful inside the walls.

I

Many responsible American citizens believe that the United States government does not really want to win the war on drugs. Even with the formation of the Drug Enforcement Agency (DEA as it is popularly called), there are more drugs on the street, and the dope gets purer and more addictive every year.

Bill O'Reilly writes in his book <u>The No Spin Zone</u> that the lucrative narcotics business for some is just too hard to control. In his book he notes:

1.   There are in excess of 10 million "heavy drug users" in the United States.

2.   Approximately 70 percent of all street crime is drug related.

3.   Approximately 70 percent of all child abuse is committed by substance abuse users (this includes those who abuse alcohol).

4.   There are more than one million DUI arrests annually in the United States.

O'Reilly opines that with numbers like these even someone high on ecstasy or crank can figure it out – Intoxication is an horrendous problem (if not a profitable) problem in America. These figures are supported by the hundreds of thousands of inmates in America currently serving time for drug-related crimes.

He summarizes in his book the basic strategies he feels are needed to control America's drug problems. First, impose coerced drug rehabilitation on all criminals who are arrested and test positive for narcotics. Second, use the U. S. military to assist the Border Control from Brownsville, Texas to Imperial Beach, California, and use the Navy to assist the Coast Guard. Third, sentence major and persistent drug dealers to banishment in far away federal penitentiaries.

In an interview with David Stoddard, a former Border Patrol supervisor and a 21-year veteran of the agency, told O'Reilly:

1. The United States military is the best equipped, best trained and most technologically advanced search force in the world.

2. It was his experience that the mere presence of the U. S. military on the border deterred illegal aliens as well as narcotic trafficking.

3. He would put the military on the border, regain control "and deploy their numbers in strength from Brownsville, Texas, to San Diego."

In the educated counselor's classroom, alcohol abuse is rated as the major or king of all substance problems. It is legal in all fifty states and is fairly inexpensive. It is considered socially acceptable and yet alcohol is a potentially addictive drug. Many regard alcohol as the primary vehicle that leads to heavier drug abuse, addiction and criminal activities.

Alcoholics Anonymous (AA) is considered the most successful self-help group of its kind. However, its effectiveness is limited within the prison setting. It is usually attended on a voluntary basis but can be mandated by a judge during the sentencing phase. It offers "The Twelve Step Program" and "Twelve Traditions," which offer common sense values and a great deal of social value for the attendees. AA is the most well attended self-help program in the world today, offered at no cost in almost every country and every language in the world.

As inmates return to a clean and sober lifestyle in prison, many of them regain a desire to change. The Higher Power spiritualism offered in AA, NA and CA is a priceless commodity that is extremely popular and successful inside the walls.

Chapter II

The Prison System

The current "get Tough on Crime" and the "Three Strikes" laws are very effective and have, in fact, literally created a "Prison State" within the State of California. As a result of the "Get Tough On Crime" legislation, we see offenders, many of whom are generally on a non-violent sentence brought into the system, and their numbers have immensely increased. Many of their offenses range from drug-related crimes associated with obtaining cash to buy drugs.

II

There are now 32 prisons in the state of California and five more in the planning stages as this is being written.

California's first state prison opened in 1852 aboard an old ship, The Wabon, anchored in San Pablo Bay off Port Quentin. The ship housed up to 150 male and female inmates.

According to the California Department of Corrections, inmates worked during the day to build the main prison. At night the inmates were locked in the hold of the old hulk. After two years, the inmates moved into San Quentin, known then as the "Old Spanish Block." The state took permanent control of the prison in 1861 from a private lessee.

Folsom, the state's second prison, was begun in 1858. The prison opened in 1880, twenty-two years after construction had started. New prisons followed as California's population rapidly progressed. During the 1970's, the inmate population stabilized and even seemed to decline. No new prisons were constructed during this time.

However, in the 1980's, changes in legislation and a general "get tough" campaign contributed to a large jump in the number of inmates. Within a span of five years, between 1980 and 1985, the prison population soared from 24,500 inmates to more than 50,000 according to CDC statistics. By the spring of 1991, the inmate population again doubled to top 100,000 prisoners housed in the system. By the middle of 1993 these numbers had increased to more than 114,000.

Again, according to the CDC, the mass influx of inmates severely stressed a prison system that in 1980 was designed for only 23,500 inmates. The department responded with a massive construction program. Bond issues authorized almost three billion dollars for prison construction in 1981, 1984, 1986, 1988 and 1990. Additional lease purchase and general fund distributions pushed the total to nearly $5 billion for new prison construction. This trend still continues today and plays a prominent role in the state's budget.

The Director of the California Department of Corrections is appointed by the governor to manage the state's prison, parole and community-based systems. Aggressive new and ongoing training is provided throughout the system, according to the state, but it falls way short of being in all prisons and very short in serving all inmates. Presently both men and women are being incarcerated for very lengthy terms. Almost 80% of all prison offenses involves drug abuse.

The current "Get Tough on Crime" and the "Three Strikes" laws are very effective and have, in fact, literally created a "Prison State" within the state of California. As a result of the "Get Tough on Crime" legislation we see offenders, many of whom are generally on a non-violent sentence brought into the system, and their numbers have climbed immensely. Many of their offenses range from drug-related crimes associated with obtaining cash to buy drugs. On any given day in California, about 159,000 inmates are in prison and another 116,000 parolees are struggling to stay out of prison!

This rise in numbers has created a "Graying Population" as prisoners age and pose new challenges for a somewhat geriatric group. Major accommodations, such as wheelchairs and accessibility ramps (even solitary confinement is wheelchair friendly), and major modifications as to how institutions deliver healthcare to its population have been introduced. Due to the many years of substance abuse and other major health risk factors, many older inmates require huge amounts of medications.

In California's Chino State Prison, one inmate was reported to be on a regimen of 15 different prescribed medications on a daily basis. This is obviously very costly and reflects the level of medical care that the state is required to provide to its ailing inmates.

Chapter III

Prison Programs and How They Work

The most important missed opportunity in prison is a glaring lack of comprehensive vocational and academic training for the inmates. Incarceration without education is just doing time.

As designed, the Civil Addict Program is a profoundly well-thought-out positive prison program. Though it can be used as a foundation, it needs far more expansion in the population and in the community.

III

The most important missed opportunity in prison is a glaring lack of comprehensive vocational and academic training for the inmates.

Incarceration without education is "just doing time." Warehousing inmates is a very graphic, yet very accurate description for the way most inmates spend their time. Lying or sitting on bunk beds in mostly crowded conditions is not advantageous for either mental or physical stimulation. Indeed, it tends to lead to boredom, angst, hostility, hopelessness and endless stress.

In 1961, the California legislature enacted the original law establishing the California Civil Addict Program, providing for the commitment and treatment of narcotic addicts and persons in imminent danger of becoming addicted.[1] The new law provided for the rehabilitation of such persons under the custody and administrative direction of the California Department of Corrections.

The Civil Addict Program is a two-phase program, which consists of the institutional phase and the outpatient/parole phase. Individuals committed to the program are confined to the California Rehabilitation Center in Norco, California, during the inpatient phase of the program. A variety of programs have been offered to the addict while he or she is confined. These programs included vocational and academic education, self-help groups and work assignments. When the inmate is released to outpatient status or civil addiction parole, the

[1] California Penal Code, Title 7, part 3.

program provides for supervision, control and anti-narcotic testing as well. Frequent anti-narcotic testing allows for the early detection of potential drug abuse.

The program also provides for immediate intervention and prompt return to confinement of those parolees who revert to narcotic use or otherwise violate the conditions of release and parole. In addition, parolees who revert to narcotic use may turn themselves into their parole agent or seek admission to the California Treatment Center for a limited placement for a maximum of 60 days. Many of these addicts have taken advantage of this provision, rather than risk becoming strung out and returning to a life of crime to support their drug habits.

The period of parole for a Civil Addict could extend up to three years, plus one year for any time spent in custody as a parole violator. However, these parolees could be considered for early discharge from their parole if they abstained from narcotics and otherwise have complied with their parole conditions for a specified period of time and depending upon their status when they were placed on parole.

The Director of Corrections has the authority to exclude certain persons from the Civil Addict Program because of "excessive criminality or for other relevant reasons."[2] Suitability for Civil Addict Program:

- Primary Problem – Drug Abuse

- Manageable Within Program Resources

[2] Title 15, California Code.

- Trafficking In Narcotics Minimal

- Over Age 18

- Availability For Civil Addict Program

The Civil Addict Program was designed to provide information to use in solving real problems, both in the institution and in the community. All civil commitments must complete this program before they can be considered for release.

Many of the inmates are school dropouts and some are illiterate. The law mandates that any individual testing below the sixth grade level, must be assigned to an academic program. The median grade placement level for the inmate population is the eighth grade. This, in spite of the fact, that we are the richest most creative country and remaining super-power in the world! California ranks fifth in the world, on a global economy scale.

Participants receive high school diplomas and elementary school certificates through the local unified school districts. CRC has an excellent GED program and awards high school diplomas to some 300 inmates per year. For this, they deserve tremendous credit as the classes are fairly difficult, and the reading comprehension and prior class work is so low.

Vocational training is highly recommended for prisons as the school drop-out level for most inmates is so high. The bulk of the population is under-educated and without job training. Vocational courses in upholstery, drafting, automotive repair, building maintenance, word processing, offset printing, x-ray technology, office machine repair and secretarial work provide individuals with skills to get a job. CRC offered all of the above training at one time. Over the years it has suffered budget cuts and lack of appreciation at the Department of Corrections for education for the inmates within the framework of the prison system.

The California Rehabilitation Center has created six Therapeutic Communities at CRC. Each Community carries a caseload of approximately 100 inmates who are segregated from the rest of the prison population. The inmates spend one-half of their day "programming" in academic classrooms which are facilitated by an approved treatment center. Non-profit companies have bid on the project and have been accepted with full staff at CRC. The second half of the inmates' day is spent in an actual prison job as a porter, clerk, cafeteria worker, et cetera.

The California Division of Forestry operates a 62-man forestry camp on the grounds of CRC. The individuals assigned there are engaged in conservation work and are subject to call throughout the state for fire suppression and flood control.

Philosophy, Goals and Objectives[3]

Although the Narcotic Addict Evaluation Authority has no statutory responsibility for the administration of the Civil Addict Program, by the broad powers vested in the Board, it is able to indirectly set policy that affects the treatment, parole and rehabilitation of the civilly committed addict. The Authority is an integral part of the Civil Addict Program and as such, is concerned with the needs of the total program.

The Narcotic Addict Evaluation Authority, in conjunction with the Department of Corrections, believes that all segments of the Civil Addict Program must work cooperatively to reach the goals of this program. These goals are:

1.   The protection of society.

2.   The prevention and control of narcotic addiction.

3.   The rehabilitation of the narcotic addict.

It is the foremost aim of the Board to exercise proper control of the civil addict population by considering what is best for the addict at the least expense to the taxpayer. This can best be accomplished by maintaining the individual in the institution for such time as is necessary to ensure that there will be a reasonably safe return to the community, and to retain him/her in the community as long as the individual does not present an immediate threat to himself/herself or others. The philosophy and policy of the Authority that governs its

---

[3] California Code of Regulations. Title 15, Prevention and Corrections.

actions through granting release to outpatient/parole status, revocation of outpatient/parole status, or "suspend-reinstatements" directly affect the work of the Department of Corrections. The decisions made by the Authority, the reason these decisions are made, and the manner in which they are communicated to the individual may have a positive or negative effect not only on his/her adjustment in the institution and ultimate rehabilitation, but also on the entire Civil Addict Program. In like manner, the decisions of the Board relate directly to the maintenance of community harmony and preservation of social order.

The Narcotic Addict Evaluation Authority is not only cognizant of its responsibility to the public, but also of its responsibility to the civilly committed addict. Board policy stimulates that each case be judged on its individual merit, without prejudice. The Authority has always informed the individual of its decision at the close of the hearing. In addition, if release is denied, the person is provided with the reasons for the denial in writing. In those cases where an outpatient's/parolee's case is being reviewed for violation which may lead to a return to the institution, the Board takes into consideration all of the factors involved, including any correspondence received from relatives or other interested parties. If the individual is ordered to return to the institution, he/she may contest the charges made against him/her at a revocation hearing which is conducted by an impartial hearing officer who reports his/her findings to the Authority. In the event good cause is not found to return the person to the institution, the person is immediately released back into outpatient/parole status. If good cause is found, the person will remain in the facility until such time as the Warden certifies that the person is ready for release consideration or is considered on an Annual Review and the Board grants release to the outpatient/parole status.

The law allows the Narcotic Addict Evaluation Authority discretion in deciding whether an individual should be returned to the institution or continued in outpatient/parole status. The Authority is aware that narcotic addiction is usually a life-long problem, and individuals who revert to narcotics use must be controlled in order to protect the public from the crimes they commit. Therefore, the Authority places much emphasis on providing sufficient external controls; such as, frequent testing while on outpatient/parole status, and interrupting narcotic use before it becomes necessary for the addict to commit crimes to support his/her habit.

As designed, the Civil Addict Program is a profoundly well-thought out, positive prison program. Though it can be used as a strong foundation, it needs far more expansion in the population and in the community.

Chapter IV

Prison Programs and Why Some Fail

Aftercare (or after prison) has been and still remains the most overlooked ingredient of the inmate curriculum.

More education is needed inside and following prison. Whether vocational or academic, all inmates need education – No! Make that EDUCATION!!! – and if their home is no longer welcome to them after parole, treatment centers and sober living houses can fill the bill.

IV

After care (or after prison) has been and still remains the most over-looked ingredient of the inmate curriculum.

It is inevitably the excellent, well-conceived after-care program that gets cut from the prisons' budgets because it is not a security issue. It also does not rank in the same category as food and clothing. But many experts in the criminal justice field will agree that after care has definitely become a life or death issue for thousands of inmates paroled from prisons across the country and throughout the world.

A long understood dynamic by judges, psychologists, police and prison personnel, is that the road to prison is a long roller coaster ride through the dark side. Family, friends, loved ones, jobs and personal self-esteem are all usually lost by the wayside when along the path the individual is transformed from individual to inmate. Personal health usually takes a major toll as heroine, cocaine and alcohol abuse all attack the basic functioning of the abuser turned criminal.

Drug abuse attacks the teeth, joints, eyes, personal hygiene and eating habits as well as all of the body organs. The brain is abused to the point of becoming bruised and soggy and begins to send mixed messages to a tired, aching and sleep-deprived body. The Alcoholic/ drug-addicted person literally loses control of his/her ability to control thought processes as well as memory and past value systems.

Proposition 36 became law in California in 2001 and has already had a huge impact on the prison population. Historically, California's prison population consisted of about 30 percent women. However, since Proposition 36, the prison inmates housed at CRC have been dramatically affected to the point that there are few women at this facility. Why is this? The law provides that first and second-time offenders who have proven alcohol and/or drug problems are allowed to be assigned to a treatment center rather than a prison. A ninety-day to six month assignment to a treatment center in lieu of a prison term has become a popular sentencing alternative. What a great concept! No prison record and a lot of education! It works and the cost to the taxpayer is incredibly reduced.

An after-care pre-release type of program can make remarkable change in an individual's time in prison. Focused substance abuse classes; homework assignments to take to the dorm; play-acting and professional group training in the prison classroom is time extremely well spent in prison instead of "just doing time."

The California Rehabilitation Center in Norco, California, has made a long and continuous attempt to be the premier and only state designated major treatment prison in the State of California. In many areas they have achieved noble and excellent work. Other prisons around the state have lesser programs in substance abuse and vocational efforts and fall far short of serving the inmates.

Once again, budget problems are a major obstacle. As of this writing, a sitting governor has been recalled for budget overspending. Prison layoffs are at an unprecedented rate while the inmate population continues to grow.

CRC has an inmate population of close to 5,000 and is classified as a Level 2 prison. Level 3 and Level 4 are where the more violent inmates are sent. These prisons have a high risk factor with the criminal population, and all of the inmates are assigned cells. CRC is a converted naval hospital, and inmates sleep in open dorms of approximately 100 inmates per dorm with attached bathrooms, shower facilities and a day room for meetings or group activities.

CRC has two libraries, one for the men and one for the women. Medical facilities are also located on both the men and women's sides. Visiting areas, walking areas and workout areas without iron for pumping are also available. Inmates receive three meals per day prepared by a dietician, and TV lounge areas are located in specific areas.

So what is wrong with this program and all the other prisons in California and probably throughout the nation? The answer is that more education is needed. Whether vocational or academic, all inmates need education, no make that EDUCATION!

It is absolutely endemic to the success of the inmate and the institution. Again, incarceration without education is just doing time. Warehousing inmates creates boredom, rage, loss of self-esteem, hostility and loathing for both self and the institution.

The California Rehabilitation Center[4]

The California Rehabilitation Center is located in Norco, California and is a correctional institution operated by the Department of Corrections. The purpose

---

[4] CRC Intake Manual.

of the institution is to provide control, confinement, employment, education and treatment for civilly committed drug abusers. In addition, the facility houses felon commitments who have been sent to State Prison. At the present time, the institution is operated by a staff of over 1,100 personnel and has the capacity for approximately 4,000 males and 800 females (who are housed in separated units). The integrity of the institution's perimeter is maintained by a double fence, armed officers who are stationed in strategically located watch towers and an armed outside patrol sergeant.

Persons committed from northern counties are received by prisons located in northern California and transferred to the California Rehabilitation Center. Commitments from southern counties are received directly at the California Rehabilitation Center, and both northern and southern commitments are immediately assigned to reception dormitories for initial processing. The first week includes a complete physical examination. In addition, the Test of Adult Basic Education (TABE) is administered to measure academic levels. Initial interviews are conducted and tentative plans are made to determine which program the individual will be placed into.

There are 53 dormitories (42 male and 11 female). The basic program unit is the dormitory unit supervised by a correctional officer. The individual participates in the classification process and his or her desires and needs are taken into consideration in formulating the program plan. Currently each Correctional Counselor 1 has a caseload of approximately 150 individuals comprised of both civil commitments and felon commitments. Currently, the program is structured to focus on preparing an individual for release back to the community with the skills and preparation which would enable the person to remain free.

CIVIL COMMITMENT EDUCATION PROGRAM

This program is designed to provide information for civil addict commitments to use in solving real problems both in the institution and in the community. All new civil commitments must complete this program before they can be considered for release.

EDUCATIONAL AND VOCATIONAL TRAINING

Many of the individuals are school dropouts and some are illiterate. The law mandates that any individual testing below the sixth grade level must be assigned to an academic program. The median grade placement level for the population is eight. Participants receive high school diplomas and elementary school certificates through the local Corona-Norco Unified School District. In many instances vocational training is a necessity since the bulk of the population is under-educated and without job training. Vocational courses in upholstery, drafting, automotive repair, building maintenance, word processing, offset printing, x-ray technology, dry cleaning, electronic technology, office machine repair and secretarial work provide individuals with skills to get a job.

RELIGION

The California Rehabilitation Center has an active religious program designed to assist the individual develop more socially skilled, wholesome values. A full-time Catholic Priest and Protestant Chaplain as well as a part-time Jewish Rabbi and Muslim

Minister are actively involved in encouraging participation in the religious programs at the Center. Visiting chaplains of other denominations also provide services.

Chapter V

The Corrections Counselor:Operation Bootstrap

The Correctional Counselors work for years without a clear, functional education and training program of what they are supposed to do as counselors. Consequently, their work is boring and uneventful. The counselors stand out as the weakest link in the treatment chain.

The Department of Corrections should provide an additional incentive by reimbursing the employees' cost for all or part of educational courses which lead to certification in counseling at the Community College level. These programs are excellent and very affordable for well-paid counselors currently performing without portfolio.

The prisons have Corrections Officers and some have Correction Counselors.

Unfortunately, the Correction Counselor Program is usually a disaster in all prisons, and as structured, a waste of taxpayers' money. The problem, once again, is education: actually the lack thereof. Correctional Counselors are paid very well and are unionized. The union has done great work for them in the area of salaries, bonuses, vacation schedules, generous overtime pay and one of the best benefit packages and retirement plans in the whole nation!

Correction Counselors generally work their way up through the ranks, many years after serving as Correctional Officers. Often, their mentality is mired in their earlier training and their approach to their job is based on their experiences acquired as Correctional Officers and crowd control methods learned in Baton 101.

Many of these counselors have done little to prepare themselves to be successful in their new role. Few have training in Alcohol and Drug Studies; little or no training in Victimology or even a class in Criminal Justice! The same GED or high school diploma suffices as education requirement to qualify. The ascension from Corrections Officer to Correction Counselor goes—get them out of the rain and the wind, out of the towers and they don't have to work the swing or graveyard shifts any longer. All that they get to prepare themselves for their new role is some on-the-job training, usually through the IST office, which specializes in corrections skills. The CCI works for years without a clear, functional education and training program of what they are supposed to do as counselors.

Consequently, their work is boring and uneventful. Few usually leave or quit their new assignment because the pay is excellent and the benefits are great. Most correctional officers or counselors function with a GED or high school diploma. Very, very few have college credits or (God forbid) a college degree. It is just too comfortable the way it is set up, and no one rocks the boat. The union is in control of almost everyone classified as staff who works at the prison. Wardens, deputy wardens and associate wardens usually have an AA or bachelor's degree and receive excellent compensation for their work. All rank and file employees belong to the union.

The education department staff are usually degreed, but most accounting staff, procurement specialists, personnel, prison kitchen managers and other staff rank very low in the education area. Most have worked their way up through the system to obtain their positions and over the years have become very competent in their jobs.

The counselors, however, stand out as the weakest link in the treatment chain, and there is not legitimate reason for this. Here is our simple recommendation to remedy part of the problem: *Education, Education, Education!*

All correctional officers desiring to become counselors and leave working in the towers, the fences, and the shift changes, should be offered an incentive to educate themselves for the counseling positions they seek. We have to raise the bar for many of the prisoners that are being "counseled" and in many cases have a higher education level than their counselors. This requirement should be mandatory for anyone acting in the counselor position.

The Community Colleges are the best place to start. Tuition is still very inexpensive, currently at $11.00 to $18.00 per unit in California's excellent community college system. Hence, $54.00 for a class semester and another $100.00 for the course text (even cheaper if purchased used at the college bookstore) is all that is needed to start. The instructors and professors at the community college level are incredibly competent. They usually process a minimum of a master's degree or are doctorates in their field. The adjunct instructor staff must have a bachelor's degree and usually possess credentials and years of experience in their particular subject matter.

These instructors go through a specific interviewing process by the community college district office, as well as the community college department director. A credential in Criminal Justice, Victimology, Alcohol and Drug Studies and Human Services Generalist normally comprises 33 college units each. Then, for a modest outlay, these candidates can attain an academic background and credentials in the specific area in the field of their choice. After the *peripheral* units of one full curriculum for one credential (i.e., Criminal Justice) is completed, it is not again required for additional credentials at the college in the same department group.

The core group of classes (and these are usually one-half of the total class units needed) normally amount to 12 to 16 units. Thus, this is really a big help to the cost-conscious student in that each additional credential will only cost the student the core tuition and the requisite textbooks. Thus, an additional credential could cost less than what it cost for the initial credential.

The Department of Corrections in most states is not known for its generosity or awareness when it comes to promoting education among the prison staff. This is not only anachronistic, but a real blunder in the prison's ability to retain counselors who are not only well trained for their work, but current in the ongoing methodology and procedures being taught in the Human Services departments of the community colleges across the nation.

Confucius once said:

Pain makes man think; Thought makes man wise; Wisdom can bring happiness. Why not spread education around at a massive level when thousands of our citizens are being incarcerated? One must have training to teach. The Department of Corrections literally dummies down their correctional counselors when they do not provide and make mandatory a training system and academic requirements to meet the needs of the counselors.

To begin this program, current correctional counselors could be grandfathered into their positions with the proviso that they complete the requirements for certification in one or more of the counseling curriculum we have discussed. However, new appointees should be required to have completed at least one or more credentials as a prerequisite to apply for the position if they are not degreed.

The Department of Corrections could provide an additional stimulus by reimbursing its employees for a part or all of the cost incurred for the cost of the certification. The benefit to the department would be a motivated counselor interested in the position as an occupation rather than a promotion. And the programs would furnish added resources to the counselors and to the inmate population they teach.

Chapter VI

After Care: Community Based Organizations and Faith and Spiritual Communities

President George W. Bush has stated that faith-based charities helping homeless and displaced Americans would be a part of his domestic agenda.

We have included an entire explanation in this chapter of how these Communities, made up of churches and sober living houses, can supply refuge, safety and a place to get started for those parolees and others attempting to assimilate back into society.

A complete program is offered relative to this chapter on "How To Start and Operate Your Own Sober Living House."

President George W. Bush stated in his presidential campaign speeches, and since, that faith-based charities helping homeless and displaced Americans would be a part of his domestic agenda.

Even with all our wars in Afghanistan and Iraq consuming his attention, the president has made certain this is still a priority item and has indeed become a part of the 2003 – 2004 budget. The 2002 National Institute of Drug and Alcohol (NIDA) report, prepared in Washington, D.C. is such important, knowledgeable reading, we have enclosed it in its full format for your enlightenment and as a handy resource for your possible desire to know more about this great work currently happening in America and perhaps to even get you involved in it in your community. The "No Child Left Behind" Education Act the president has had approved by congress and a compassionate program for the homeless can help thousands of parolees, and, of course, many others to never experience prison as an inmate. This is prescribed tax dollars doing excellent work for our American citizenry. It certainly helps to take advantage of the greatly missed opportunity in prisons by keeping people out of prison. As President Bush stated in his State of the Union address, one mentor, one person can change a life forever, and he urged each of us to be that person.

It is obvious that the CRC program and all other prison programs will be severely set back by this recession. But, as usual, it is a sure bet that it will bounce back. It will take some time, but when it does, new measures must be put in place.

1.   All prisons should have strong substance abuse programs.

2.   All prisons should have basic literacy programs that lead to a GED accomplishment.

3.   All prisons should have at least some basic vocational education programs that lead to job skills.

4.   All prisons should have a strong pre-release program that prepares inmates for assimilation into the community – this is called **After-care**.

An inmate is considered a success when he or she does not return to prison. After-care is the solution to the recidivism (re-incarceration) problem.

Prisons should not allow:

- **<u>Conjugal Visits</u>** – Inmates have been sent to prison to think about what they have been doing wrong. Sex and the sexual acts are a great distraction to this focus. Men inmates have a history of being mentally and physically abusive to an approved sex partner as their expectations become very exaggerated while they are in confinement. They use their sex partners as tools and are very demanding of them. Many of their sex partners have been abused and in some cases arrested for bringing in contraband (some of which are illegal drugs) concealed in their bodies.

- **<u>Pumping Iron</u>** – Normal workouts, including running and brisk walking are necessary and beneficial to the inmates and should be encouraged. Pumping iron can create monsters. Studies have shown that police departments throughout the country oppose inmates pumping iron inside as some parolees are so strong that as many as six trained uniform officers can "barely bring them down." This type of inmate usually becomes meaner, angrier and tougher during incarceration and is a larger threat to society. Many states, like California, have outlawed pumping iron in the prisons and weights have been removed. This type of inmate is even a greater threat to commit domestic violence upon his family members; even more so, to law enforcement officials and to other good people who do not deserve to be confronted by an out-of-control parolee with a definite edge, honed in a tax-funded prison.

- **<u>To Create and Attend Nation of Islam Meetings</u>** – Generally speaking, most inmates do not understand the Koran, Jihad or any other of the Muslim teaching. They interpret a message of violence and disruption that the Koran does not say or advocate. Unfortunately, becoming a Muslim inside the prison is akin to joining the Mob and fosters violence rather than working against it.

- **<u>White Supremacy Groups</u>** – These groups are not a religion and function very much like Hitler's Youth Groups as prejudiced, misguided tough-guy predators on other races in prison. They should be disbanded and the members sent to Level 3 and Level 4 prisons. There, they can be restrained better and subjected to more supervision while almost in constant lock down.

41

As all inmates are annually reviewed, they do have a chance to repent and get better!

- **<u>The Provocative and Confrontational</u>** – It doesn't take a rocket scientist or a brain surgeon to realize something is amiss in the persistent, aggressive malcontents. If nothing is ever right for him or her on the outside, it would necessarily not be okay on the inside. Inmates must be kept busy. Training, working and group function involvement should always be mandatory in every prison. People don't become inmates overnight and they are not going to change their behavior right away…maybe never. The seed must be constantly replanted and in the end, the inmate cannot be allowed to ruin the class, group, training movie or whatever activity at the expense of the other inmates. Only the inmate can change him/her self. If the inmate will not, he/ she must be moved. Only trained, educated staff can recommend and make these decisions.

Chapter VII

What Is Needed Now and Why It Must Work.

Mental health problems, renewed drug addiction and alcohol abuse relapse can all happen to the parolee after time spent in prison...especially following a prolonged sentence.

For those who are not rearrested, trouble on the job, trouble on the home front and even trouble on the street can create further mental stress which is usually vented in the guise of belligerence.

Until prisons begin to really invest in strong correction counselor education and training, the blind will continue to lead the deaf.

VII

An idle mind is the devil's workshop. Inmates need to be kept busy; whether they think so or not.

Prison incarceration over a long period of time can result in serious mental health and drug addiction problems for many inmates trying to parole successfully into their communities.

Severe alcohol abuse relapse and the inability to function well on the outside can lead to parole violation and a trip back to prison. For those who are not rearrested, trouble on the job; the home front or even off the street can create further mental strain which is usually expressed in belligerence. Again, we see that incarceration without any form of education is just doing time.

Until prisons begin to really invest in strong correction counselor education and training programs, the blind will continue to try and show the way by talking to the deaf.

The Betty Ford Center in Palm Desert, California, is a classic example of what works in substance abuse treatment. But, alas, not everyone can afford the price tag. Also, the Ford programs are designed for individuals experiencing problems with substance abuse, not usually criminality. But the "Cycle of Addiction"[5] spares no one.

The prison offers a captive audience who can become an asset to the community equipped with a GED if he or she does not possess a high school diploma, and also a credential that acknowledges they have earned a learned skill. Not every inmate is going to be qualified for, or necessarily desire what we are presenting here. But we recommend if the inmate has the basic intelligence and is psychologically able to do this that they be mandated for training at classification.

The Department of Corrections must display an honest effort of sending qualified representatives to the legislature to secure adequate budgets for dynamic programs. California will be strong again and like the incredibly successful GI Bill from World War II, we must present fresh, positive and rehabilitative history to our legislators.

As the Negro College Fund motto goes, "A mind is too great to waste." While our citizens are doing time, it should be productive. American adults who have strayed are still American adults. Many have served honorably in our military. Many are still loved and prayed for by their loved ones.

Hire teachers. We don't need new prisons! Education, handled wisely, is an investment for a continued, civilized country. We have the resources to do things like this. We just need to check the country's conscience more often. Drug dealers operate at night and in the shadows. They can usually gross more money in one month than their fathers made in a lifetime.

Proposition 36 in California has given us a strong and conclusive proof what human service educators and counselors have been telling us for years; Treatment Works! "Fighting drugs is not like working with an on-time railroad train. The strategies meet resistance and must be changed or modified at different times for different reasons," says four-star general Barry McCaffrey, former U.S. drug czar.

It has been written that morality and religion are the bedrock foundation for clean politics. Idealism, with principles can bring positive progress to the inmate population. Too harsh, too tough or too touchy, too feely as they say in the substances abuse treatment centers must be avoided as balanced, knowledgeable common sense is brought to the classroom table or lectern to deal with inmates. The inmate knows quicker than anyone when he is being "conned."

Over 300 inmates per year, men and women, receive their GED at CRC after focused, not too easy, classroom education taught by state credentialed instructors. Motivation, self-esteem and self-confidence are instilled in a fairly unconfident group as they work hard to change themselves and prepare for release back to society.

As mentioned earlier in this book, focused caring for our fellow human being is a noble attempt by a very caring group of American teachers to improve the parolees' chances for success on the outside.

Parole terms should be as close to one year as possible to allow parolees to get out of the system and move on with their lives. Long-term parole, unless very necessary, is too strict, too redundant and too demoralizing in most instances for the low-income and usually low self-esteemed parolee. "Done the crime; served the time; now let me go" is a common complaint of the parolees. When one thinks about that expression, it not only makes sense; it is very American. Opportunity is certainly missed when an inmate is not really rehabilitated;

anger is stuffed down further in the gut; and more wasted tax dollars have turned into wasted time served.

TARGETED OUTREACH | **Community-Based Organizations and Faith and Spiritual Communities**

Community-Based Organizations and Faith and Spiritual Communities

In the year 2000, an estimated 14 million people in the U.S. were current users of illicit drugs, meaning they used an illicit drug during the month prior to being interviewed. The number of heavy drinkers—individuals who consumed five or more drinks on the same occasion on at least five different days in the past 30 days—was estimated at 12.6 million.[1] An estimated one in four children lives in a family where a parent drinks too much.[2] Given these numbers, there is no denying that drug and alcohol abuse affects every facet of American life. Consider these additional facts:[3]

- There are more deaths, illnesses, and disabilities each year from drug and alcohol problems than from any other preventable health condition.

- Drug and alcohol use and addiction can result in family violence and mistreatment of children. Drug and alcohol addiction issues are factors in the placement of more than three-quarters of children entering foster care.

- Public safety is greatly affected by drug and alcohol problems in terms of increased crime, motor vehicle accidents, and violence.

- Children who are raised in homes where drug and alcohol problems are present are at much higher risk for developing their own problems in the future. Young adults are most likely to use alcohol, tobacco, and illicit drugs.

The good news is that community-based organizations and faith and other spiritual communities, especially those most interested in addressing the needs of families, can have a very positive impact on the problem. Here's why:

- For six out of 10 Americans, religious faith is the most important influence in their lives, and for eight out of 10, religious beliefs provide comfort and support.[4]

- Spirituality is an important part of recovery for many individuals with drug or alcohol problems.[5]

- Teens who never attend religious services are at above average risk for drug and alcohol problems, while weekly and more frequent attendees have a lower than average risk. Furthermore, the proportion of a teen's friends who attend religious services appears more relevant to the teen's risk score than even the teen's own degree of religious attendance.[6]

- There is evidence that social support from friends and outside influences can moderate the effects of a family history of drug and alcohol problems.[7]

- Children who coped effectively with the trauma of growing up in families affected by alcoholism often relied on the support of a non-alcoholic parent, stepparent, grandparent, teachers, or others when they were growing up.[8]

- Factors that have been cited in fostering student ability to resist drugs include positive peer affiliations, bonding/involvement in school activities, relationships with caring adults, opportunities for school success and responsible behavior, and the availability of drug-free activities.[9]

Making a Difference: What Can I Do?

1. **Know the facts about addiction, treatment, and the recovery process.** Recent advances in medical science have proven that addiction is a chronic illness that can be successfully treated. In fact, treatment for addiction is as successful as treatments for other chronic health conditions, such as diabetes, hypertension, and asthma.[12] Recovery from drug addiction can be a long-term process and may require multiple episodes of treatment. It is critical to understand that occasional reoccurrence of use is not necessarily a sign of failure, but can be an inherent part of the journey to long-term abstinence.[13]

2. **Be mindful of special populations.** Drug and alcohol use among various racial/ethnic groups is quite comparable to that of the mainstream population, yet these groups may be less inclined to receive or seek out treatment. Reasons include: the tendency to underutilize health care services in general, addiction treatment being no exception; lower economic status and the often associated lack of health insurance coverage; lack of geographic access; lack of culturally competent treatment services; and firmly entrenched cultural beliefs and attitudes about addiction and recovery, which often stigmatize alcohol and drug abuse and those in recovery.[14]

   Youth, older adults, people with disabilities or co-occurring mental illnesses, and individuals of various sexual orientations may face special hurdles in acknowledging their drug and alcohol problems and dealing with them effectively. Faith-based and other spirituality-based organizations often serve as a safe haven for these individuals. If representatives and members of these groups are sensitized to the needs of special populations who may have drug and alcohol problems, the likelihood that these individuals will find support and encouragement in addressing their addictions is greatly increased. Religious organizations should also be mindful of the importance of referring people to mental health/substance abuse professionals when needed.

3. **Build effective community partnerships.** To address drug and alcohol problems at the local level, community stakeholders must join forces. Hundreds of anti-drug coalitions and community-sponsored programs are aiding thousands of men, women, children, and families nationwide in preventing and reducing addiction. Their efforts include, but are by no means limited to: supporting and educating children and youth in high-stress families; providing referrals and support programs to those in recovery and their loved ones; ridding neighborhoods of drug markets; and establishing social service agencies to organize conferences and campaigns.

Community-Based Organizations and Faith and Spiritual Communities *(cont.)* **TARGETED OUTREACH**

A recent report outlined the six critical components of effective community anti-drug coalitions. They are: clearly stated goals; broad-based membership; strong leadership; diversified funding sources; training; and impact evaluation.[15] Given this description, community-based organizations and faith-based and other spiritually defined organizations are equipped and have a responsibility to play an integral part in the development and sustenance of any community-based coalition effort, as facilitators, participants, sponsors, or all of the above.

4. **Never underestimate the power of the family.** Community-based organizations and faith-based as well as spirituality-based organizations serve not only individuals, but also entire families. As such, they are in a unique position to identify families in crisis, and to encourage families to work together to solve problems. Additionally, they can readily serve as a means of support to all the members of a family. It is critical for these organizations to recognize the tremendously positive impact that family can have on the willingness of the individual with a drug or alcohol problem to get help and to maintain abstinence. Support family-focused treatment of addiction in your community.

5. **Become a recognized and trusted resource.** Find out what local support groups, treatment centers, family-oriented community action groups, and self-help recovery programs are available to assist your members and members of your local community who are dealing with drug or alcohol problems. Circulate literature directing people to sources of assistance. Provide a contact name of someone in your organization who can serve as a resource for confidential guidance and referral information.

Making a Difference: How Can I Focus My Efforts during *Recovery Month*?

Recovery Month is celebrated each year during the month of September. It is a time to focus on creating solutions to the problems we all face as a result of drug and alcohol addiction. Each year, a theme is chosen that serves as a rallying cry for the thousands of individuals and organizations involved in the national effort. This year's theme is *"Join the Voices of Recovery: A Call to Action."* As a community-based organization, faith-based or other spirituality-based organization you are encouraged to participate in this year's observance. No matter how large or small your effort, you can take pride in knowing you made a contribution. Here are some thoughts to get you started planning for this year's month-long celebration and for the months that follow:

1. **Educate your staff.** If your staff members and volunteers are already well-versed in how to identify families and children who are dealing with addiction problems, then you are to be congratulated. September 2002 is a time to schedule a refresher in-service training session to make sure everyone is up to speed. If training in this area has not been a priority to date, *Recovery Month* is a great time to get started. A local treatment provider or counseling expert would be only too happy to join you for a brown-bag lunch or half-day workshop to guide your staff members and volunteers on how to be effective when assisting individuals who live with addiction in their daily lives.

2. **Use your newsletter or weekly bulletin to reach out.** Make mention in your organization's newsletter or weekly bulletin that September is *Recovery Month*. Write an article to provide encouragement and hope to individuals with drug and alcohol problems and their families. Assure them that your organization is there to assist them and provide guidance on where they can turn for help.

3. **Set aside talk time.** Allocate time during *Recovery Month* and periodically throughout the year to provide confidential religious, spiritual, or other counseling to individuals and families struggling with addiction in their lives. Promote specific dates and times when you and/or an expert in the field of addiction treatment and recovery will be available. It may be necessary to ask a counselor from a local treatment facility to join you in this effort to ensure any questions that come up can be adequately addressed.

4. **Schedule a service or Community Forum.** Schedule a religious or spiritual service or sponsor a Community Forum in September to discuss the toll drug and alcohol addiction is taking on your community and what can be done about it. If your community is already sponsoring one of many Community Forums nationwide, participate in any way that you can. Make sure to talk about the fact that treatment for drug and alcohol problems can be effective, and that recovery is possible. Then, tell people where they can go for help and that they can count on your organization as a source of support.

5. **Open your doors to recovery.** Many community-based organizations, faith-based organizations, and spirituality groups have facilities and/or headquarters of operation that can be offered free-of-charge to self-help recovery groups to house their meetings, fundraisers, and other activities. If you have not opened your doors to these groups in the past, why not use the month of September to do so?

You are encouraged to share your plans and activities for *Recovery Month* 2002 with the HHS/SAMHSA Center for Substance Abuse Treatment, your colleagues, and the general public by posting them on the official *Recovery Month* web site at http://www.samhsa.gov.

We would like to know about your efforts during *Recovery Month*. Please complete the Customer Satisfaction Form enclosed in the kit. Directions are included on the form.

For any additional *Recovery Month* materials visit our web site at http://www.samhsa.gov or call 1-800-729-6686.

Changing the Conversation

Spearheaded by the U.S. Department of Health and Human Services' Substance Abuse and Mental Health Services Administration's (SAMHSA) Center for Substance Abuse Treatment (CSAT), *Changing the Conversation: The National Treatment Plan Initiative to Improve Substance Abuse Treatment* is a nationwide effort to enhance the availability and effectiveness of treatment programs and services for drug and alcohol addiction. Dozens of experts in the treatment field, as well as community stakeholders, have been consulted to provide positive guidelines that must be addressed if *Changing the Conversation* is to reach its ultimate goal. Three of those five guidelines for positive action require participation on the part of community-based organizations and faith-based and other spiritual communities in order to affect change. They are:[10]

1. **Change Attitudes**—The stigma surrounding drug and alcohol addiction has created a tremendous barrier for millions of individuals who need treatment for their drug and alcohol problems, but who do not get it. Stigma is identified as "the most firmly entrenched obstacle for faith communities or spiritualities to overcome."[11] Faith-based groups are not alone. Negative attitudes and stigma affect not only the individual with the problem or who is in recovery, they also greatly influence families, health and wellness practitioners and providers, employers, policymakers, and many others whose decisions affect all aspects of the issue.

2. **Build Partnerships**—Combating drug and alcohol problems and enhancing the availability and effectiveness of treatment programs and services can be achieved through the combined efforts of the public and private sectors, as well as community-based organizations. Faith-based and other spiritual communities can also contribute resources, support, and expertise to foster and sustain partnerships at the local and regional levels.

3. **"No Wrong Door" to Treatment**—Community-based organizations and faith-based and other spiritual communities are often the first place families and individuals turn for assistance. **"No Wrong Door" to Treatment** calls for both public and private organizations to identify and refer individuals to appropriate treatment services.

In keeping with these three guidelines for positive action, here are some steps your organization can take to have a positive impact on alcohol and substance abuse and addiction problems in your community, and to enhance the likelihood that those you serve will receive the assistance they need to recover from their addictions.

Daniel A. O'Farrell

Sources

1   *Summary of Findings from the 2000 National Household Survey on Drug Abuse.* DHHS Publication No. (SMA) 01-3549. Rockville, MD: Office of Applied Studies, Substance Abuse and Mental Health Services Administration, 2001.

2   Grant, B.F. *Estimates of U.S. children exposed to alcohol abuse and dependence in the family. American Journal of Public Health,* January 2000, Vol. 90, No. 1, pp. 112-140.

3   *Substance Abuse: The Nation's Number One Health Problem. Key Indicators for Policy.* Princeton, NJ: Robert Wood Johnson Foundation, February 2001.

4   *Alcohol, Tobacco and Other Drug Abuse: Challenges and Responses for Faith Leaders.* DHHS Publication No. (SMA) 95-3074. Washington, DC: ES Inc. for the U.S. Department of Health and Human Services, Substance Abuse and Mental Health Services Administration, Center for Substance Abuse Treatment (Contract No. 270-91-0016), 1995.

5   ibid.

6   *National Survey of American Attitudes on Substance Abuse VI: Teens.* New York, NY: National Center on Addiction and Substance Abuse, Columbia University, February 2001.

7   *Ninth Special Report to the U.S. Congress on Alcohol and Health from the Secretary of Health and Human Services.* Bethesda, MD: U.S. Department of Health and Human Services, Public Health Service, National Institutes of Health, National Institute on Alcohol Abuse and Alcoholism, June 1997.

8   Werner, E.E. and Johnson, J.L. "The Role of caring adults in the lives of children of alcoholics." *Children of Alcoholics: Selected Readings,* Vol. 2, 2000.

9   McNamara, K.M. "Best Practices in Substance Abuse Prevention Programs." *Best Practices in School Psychology III,* A. Thomas and J. Grimes (eds.). Washington, DC: National Association of School Psychologists, 1995, pp. 369-382.

10   *Changing the Conversation: The National Treatment Plan Initiative to Improve Substance Abuse Treatment.* DHHS Publication No. (SMA) 00-3480. Rockville, MD: Center for Substance Abuse Treatment, Substance Abuse and Mental Health Services Administration, November 2000.

11   Riccio, P. "Breaking Down the Walls: Connecting Faith with Communities," in *Prevention Pipeline.* Rockville, MD: Center for Substance Abuse Prevention, July/August 1996, pp. 9-12.

12   *Principles of Drug Addiction Treatment: A Research-Based Guide.* NIH Publication No. 00-4180. Bethesda, MD: National Institutes of Health, National Institute on Drug Abuse, printed October 1999/reprinted July 2000.

13   ibid.

14   *Cultural Issues in Substance Abuse Treatment.* DHHS Publication No. (SMA) 99-3278. Rockville, MD: U.S. Department of Health and Human Services, Public Health Service, Substance Abuse and Mental Health Services Administration, 1999.

15   *"Assessing Community Coalitions."* Washington, DC: Drug Strategies, as reported in *Alcoholism and Drug Abuse Weekly,* August 20, 2001.

TARGETED OUTREACH **Community-Based Organizations and Faith and Spiritual Communities** *(cont.)* **2002**

Additional Resources

Federal Agencies

U.S. DEPARTMENT OF HEALTH AND HUMAN
SERVICES (HHS)
200 Independence Avenue, SW
Washington, DC 20201
877-696-6775 (Toll-Free)
www.dhhs.gov

HHS, Substance Abuse and Mental
Health Services Administration (SAMHSA)
5600 Fishers Lane
Parklawn Building, Suite13C-05
Rockville, MD 20857
301-443-8956
www.samhsa.gov

HHS, SAMHSA
Center for Substance Abuse Treatment
5600 Fishers Lane
Rockwall II Suite 621
Rockville, MD 20857
301-443-5052

CSAT National Helpline
800-662-HELP (800-662-4357) (Toll-Free)
800-487-4889 (TDD) (Toll-Free)
877-767-8432 (Spanish) (Toll-Free)
(for confidential information on substance
abuse treatment and referral)
www.samhsa.gov

HHS, SAMHSA
Center for Mental Health Services
5600 Fishers Lane
Parklawn Building, Room 17-99
Rockville, MD 20857
301-443-2792
www.samhsa.gov

HHS, SAMHSA
National Clearinghouse for Alcohol and Drug
Information
P.O. Box 2345
Rockville, MD 20847-2345
800-729-6686 (Toll-Free)
800-487-4889 (TDD) (Toll-Free)
877-767-8432 (Spanish) (Toll-Free)
www.health.org

U.S. DEPARTMENT OF HEALTH AND HUMAN
SERVICES (HHS)
National Institutes of Health (NIH)
9000 Rockville Pike
Bethesda, MD 20892
301-496-4000
www.nih.gov

HHS, NIH
National Institute on Alcohol Abuse
and Alcoholism
Willco Building
6000 Executive Boulevard
Bethesda, MD 20892-7003
301-496-4000
www.niaaa.nih.gov

HHS, NIH
National Institute on Drug Abuse
Office of Science Policy and Communication
6001 Executive Boulevard
Room 5213 MSC 9561
Bethesda, MD 20892-9561
301-443-1124
Telefax fact sheets: 888-NIH-NIDA (Voice) (Toll-Free)
or 888-TTY-NIDA (TTY) (Toll-Free)
www.drugabuse.gov

U.S. DEPARTMENT OF EDUCATION (ED)
400 Maryland Avenue, SW
Washington, DC 20202-6123
800-872-5327 (Toll-Free)
www.ed.gov

ED, Safe and Drug-Free Schools
400 Maryland Avenue, SW
Washington, DC 20202-6123
202-260-3954
www.ed.gov/offices/OESE/SDFS

Other Resources

4-H
1400 Independence Avenue, SW
STOP 2225
Washington, DC 20250-2225
202-720-2908
www.4-h.org

Al-Anon/Alateen
For Families and Friends of Alcoholics
Al-Anon Family Group Headquarters, Inc.
1600 Corporate Landing Parkway
Virginia Beach, VA 23454-5617
888-4AL-ANON/888-425-2666 (Toll-Free)
www.al-anon.alateen.org

Alcoholics Anonymous
475 Riverside Drive, 11th Floor
New York, NY 10115
212-870-3400
www.aa.org

Aliviane NO-AD, Inc.
7722 North Loop Road
El Paso, TX 79915
915-782-4000

American Psychological Association
750 1st Street, NE
Washington, DC 20002-4242
800-374-2724 (Toll-Free)
202-336-6123 (TTY)
www.apa.org

American Public Health Association
800 I Street, NW
Washington, DC 20001
202-777-2742 (APHA)
202-777-2500 (TTY)
www.apha.org

Association of State and Territorial
Health Officials
1275 K Street, NW, Suite 800
Washington, DC 20005
202-371-9090
www.astho.org

Big Brothers/Big Sisters of America
230 North 13th Street
Philadelphia, PA 19107
215-567-7000
www.bbbsa.org

Boys & Girls Clubs of America
1230 West Peachtree Street, NW
Atlanta, GA 30309
404-815-5700
www.bgca.org

Catholic Charities, USA
1731 King Street, Suite 200
Alexandria, VA 22314
703-549-1390
www.catholiccharitiesusa.org

Child Welfare League of America
440 1st Street, NW, 3rd Floor
Washington, DC 20001
202-638-2952
www.cwla.org

Children's Defense Fund
25 E Street, NW
Washington, DC 20001
202-628-8787
www.childrensdefense.org

TARGETED OUTREACH **Community-Based Organizations and Faith and Spiritual Communities** *(cont.)*

Church of Jesus Christ of Latter Day Saints
529 14th Street, NW, Suite 900
Washington, DC 20045
202-662-7480
www.lds.org

Community Anti-Drug Coalitions of America
901 North Pitt Street, Suite 300
Alexandria, VA 22314
800-54-CADCA/800-543-2332 (Toll-Free)
www.cadca.org

Congress of National Black Churches
National Anti-Drug Campaign
2000 L Street, NW, Suite 225
Washington, DC 20036
202-296-5657
www.cnbc.org

Connecticut Community for Addiction Recovery
465 Silas Deane Highway
Wethersfield, CT 06109
860-571-2985
www.ccar-recovery.org

General Board of Global Ministries of the
United Methodist Church
Program on Substance Abuse
110 Maryland Avenue, NE, Suite 404
Washington, DC 20002
202-548-2712
www.gbgm-umc.org

Girl Scouts of the U.S.A.
Just for Girls, 15th Floor
420 5th Avenue
New York, NY 10018-2798
800-GSUSA4U/800-478-7248 (Toll-Free)
www.girlscouts.org

Jewish Alcoholics, Chemically Dependent
Persons and Significant Others
850 7th Avenue
New York, NY 10019
212-397-4197
www.jacsweb.org

Johnson Institute
2314 University Avenue, Suite 24
St. Paul, MN 55114
651-659-9100
www.jifoundation.org

Join Together
441 Stuart Street, 7th Floor
Boston, MA 02116
617-437-1500
www.jointogether.org

Mothers Against Drunk Driving
1025 Connecticut Avenue, NW, Suite 1200
Washington, DC 20036
202-974-2497
www.madd.org

Miami Coalition for a Safe and Drug-Free
Community
University of Miami, North South Center
1500 Monza Avenue
Coral Gables, FL 33146-3027
305-284-6848
www.miamicoalition.org

National Association for Children of Alcoholics
11426 Rockville Pike, Suite 100
Rockville, MD 20852
888-55-4COAS/888-554-2627 (Toll-Free)
www.nacoa.org

National Association of Community Health
Centers
1330 New Hampshire Avenue, NW, Suite 122
Washington, DC 20036
202-659-8008
www.nachc.com

Daniel A. O'Farrell

National Association of Rural Health Clinics
426 C Street, NE
Washington, DC 20002
202-543-0348
www.narhc.org

National Association of State Alcohol
    and Drug Abuse Directors
808 17th Street, NW, Suite 410
Washington, DC 20006
202-293-0090
www.nasadad.org

National Council for Community
    Behavioral Healthcare
12300 Twinbrook Parkway, Suite 320
Rockville, MD 20852
301-984-6200
www.nccbh.org

National Council on Alcoholism
    and Drug Dependence, Inc.
20 Exchange Place, Suite 2902
New York, NY 10005
212-269-7797
800-NCA-CALL (Hope Line) (Toll-Free)
www.ncadd.org

National Families in Action
2957 Clairmont Road, Suite 150
Century Plaza II
Atlanta, GA 30329
404-248-9676
www.nationalfamilies.org

Partnership for a Drug-Free America
405 Lexington Avenue, Suite 1601
New York, NY 10174
212-922-1560
www.drugfreeamerica.org

RecoveryWorks
1954 University Avenue West, Suite 12
Saint Paul, MN 55104
651-645-1618
www.addictions.org/recoveryworks

Step One
665 West 4th Street
Winston Salem, NC 27101
336-714-2116
www.stepone.org

The Alliance Project
1954 University Avenue West, Suite 12
Saint Paul, MN 55104
651-645-1618
www.defeataddiction.org
www.recoveryadvocacy.org

Therapeutic Communities of America
1601 Connecticut Avenue, NW, Suite 803
Washington, DC 20009
202-296-3503
www.tcanet.org

White Bison
6145 Lehman Drive, Suite 200
Colorado Springs, CO 80918
719-548-1000
www.whitebison.org

Young Men's Christian Association of the U.S.A.
1701 K Street, NW, Suite 903
Washington, DC 20006
202-835-9043
www.ymca.net

Young Women's Christian Association of the USA
350 5th Avenue
Empire State Building, Suite 301
New York, NY 10118
212-273-7800
www.ywca.org

SADDLEBACK COLLEGE
HUMAN SERVICES DEPARTMENT
714-582-4731/4911

OPTION II: ALCOHOL/DRUG STUDIES CERTIFICATE

The student integrates theory and practical experience in developing skills necessary to work with the alcohol and drug abuse population, as well as families and employers of chemically dependent persons. This program combines the Human Services behavioral core, skills training and experimental learning in the field work settings.

Course	Title	Units
BEHAVIORAL		
Human Services-100	Human Services in a Changing Society	3 Units
Human Services-120	Human Development in the Social Environment	3 Units
Human Services-130	Special Population Issues	3 Units
ALCOHOL/DRUG STUDIES CORE		
Human Services-170*	Drugs and Alcohol in our Society	3 Units
Human Services-171*	Alcoholism; Intervention, Treatment and Recovery	3 Units
Human Services-172*	Physiological Effects of Alcohol and Drugs	3 Units
Human Services-175	Alcohol and Drug Education and Prevention	3 Units
Human Services-210	Client Record Documentation	1 Unit
Human Services-285*	Ethical Issues & Clients Rights	1 Unit
SKILLS (Select six units from the following)		
Human Services-140	Applied Group Leadership & Group Process	3 Units
Human Services-173	Family Counseling Approaches to Alcohol/Drug Abuse	3 Units
Human Services-174	Intervention and Referral Techniques	3 Units
Human Services-180	Program Management Techniques in Human Services	3 Units
FIELD STUDIES		
Human Services-110	Field Instruction I and Seminar I	3 Units
Human Services-150	Field Instruction II and Seminar II	3 Units
	TOTAL	**35 UNITS**

*These courses qualify for continuing education for nurses.

ASSOCIATE DEGREE: Refer to Catalog for current requirements.

Human Services Department 8-93
Health Sciences & Human Services Division, Saddleback College

SADDLEBACK COLLEGE
HUMAN SERVICES DEPARTMENT
714-582-4731/4911

OPTION VIII: VICTIMOLOGY CERTIFICATE

This option introduces students to the subject of victimization and its implications within various populations groups in contemporary American society. The Certificate is designed to prepare students to work in a variety of settings dealing with victims and their families, i.e. Victim Witness, Child Abuse Education, Orangewood and other County Programs.

Course	Title	Units
BEHAVIORAL		
Human Services-100	Human Services in a Changing Society	3 Units
Human Services-120	Human Development in the Social Environment	3 Units
or		
Human Services-130	Special Population Issues	3 Units
SKILLS (Select Nine Units Plus HS-285)		
Human Services-173*	Family Counseling Approaches to Alcohol and Drugs	3 Units
Human Services-174	Crisis Intervention and Referral Techniques	3 Units
Human Services-191	Families in the 90s; Breaking the Violence Cycle	3 Units
Human Services-266	Dysfunctional Family Systems & ACA Issues	3 Units
Human Services-285*	Ethical Issues and Clients Rights	1 Unit
CORE		
Human Services-160	Introduction to Victimology	3 Units
Human Services-265	Victim Issues and Community Resources	3 Units
Human Services-119	Introduction to the Criminal Justice System	3 Units
FIELD STUDIES		
Human Services-110	Field Instruction I and Seminar I	3 Units
Human Services-150	Field Instruction II and Seminar II	3 Units
	TOTAL	**31 Units**

*These courses qualify for continuing education for nurses.

ASSOCIATE DEGREE: Refer to catalog for current requirements.

Human Services Department 10-93
Health Sciences and Human Services Division
Saddleback College

SADDLEBACK COLLEGE
HUMAN SERVICES DEPARTMENT
714-582-4731/4911

OPTION VI: CORRECTIONS & CRIMINAL JUSTICE CERTIFICATE

The specialization in Corrections and Criminal Justice program provides the student with an introduction to the Human Services behavioral Core and Skills, and a technical area of study. Students completing the program may find employment in probation, juvenile counseling settings, California Youth Authority, and half way houses.

Course	Title	Units
BEHAVIORAL		
Human Services-100	Human Services in a Changing Society	3 Units
SKILLS		
Human Services-140	Applied Group Leadership & Group Process	3 Units
Human Services-174	Intervention and Referral Techniques	3 Units
Human Services-127	Alcohol and the Law/Training the Trainer	3 Units
OR		
Human Services-170	Drugs and Alcohol in our Society	3 Units
CORE		
Human Services-115	Introduction to Criminology	3 Units
Human Services-119	Introduction to the Criminal Justice System	3 Units
Human Services-128	Community Based Corrections	3 Units
FIELD STUDIES		
Human Services-110	Field Instruction I and Seminar I	3 Units
Human Services-150	Field Instruction II and Seminar II	3 Units
	Total	**27 Units**

ASSOCIATE DEGREE: Refer to catalog for current requirements.

Human Services Department 8-93
Health Sciences and Human Services Division
Saddleback College

SADDLEBACK COLLEGE
HUMAN SERVICES DEPARTMENT
714-582-4731/4911

OPTION I: HUMAN SERVICES GENERALIST

The Generalist Certificate is designed to provide persons with both a historical and current perspective of the basic issues within the field of Human Services. It will introduce students to the growing career options within the field, provide the student an opportunity to explore several of the Departmental options and generally provide the kind of information that will enable students to make informed decisions in regards to career direction.

Course	Title	Units
BEHAVIORAL		
HS-100	Human Services in a Changing Society	3 Units
HS-120	Human Development in the Social Environment	3 Units
HS-130	Special Population Issues	3 Units
CORE		
HS-140	Applied Group Leadership and Group Process	3 Units
HS-175	Alcohol & Drug Prevention & Education	3 Units
HS-173	Family Counseling Approaches to Alcohol/Drug	3 Units
or		
HS-266	Dysfunctional Families & ACA Issues	3 Units
ELECTIVES		
Select one three unit course from electives listed below		3 Units
FIELD STUDIES		
HS-110	Field Instruction I and Seminar I	3 Units
HS-150	Field Instruction II and Seminar II	3 Units
	TOTAL	**27 Units**

Electives: Human Services 170, 171, 172, 174, 175, 180, 191; Applied Psychology 150; Sociology 1, 2, 10, 20; Psychology 106; Women's Studies 100, 135; Special Education 112, 142, 155.

ASSOCIATE DEGREE: Refer to catalog for current requirements.

Human Services Department 8-93
Health Sciences and Human Services Division, Saddleback College

Chapter VIII

The Prison Chaplain and His Role With the Population

The role of the chaplain can be a blessing in the form of a genuine catalyst which initiates change or an apathetic barnacle that leaches off the prison.

An educated correctional counseling group, combined with Therapeutic Communities good, After-Care programs and solid chaplains are a pragmatic and brave attempt to provide the educational and spiritual benefits to these inmates who are our fellow humans in crisis.

VIII

Prisons without chaplains do not have the same degree of spiritualism and Compassion that the chaplains bring to the institution

In almost every prison, the role of the chaplain can be a blessing in the form of a genuine catalyst which initiates change or an apathetic barnacle that leaches off the prison system.

Chaplains see both the good and the bad. Too often the chaplain's role is defined by the latter. Hence, where are the stellar chaplains that have a passion for the population they serve? More often than not, the difference between the effective minister and the ineffective one is knowledge and ideology. To be more specific, the effective chaplain should have a strong calling, a vocation to serve in an institution. Hence, the chaplain's job becomes a stewardship to God. A good chaplain will realize both inmates and staff are his flock.

The ineffective chaplain is not with a stewardship but rather (he/she) is concerned with self-interest that caters to his/her ego. This type of chaplain will always sow and reap the "bitter fruit" of his own ways.

In this chapter we attempt to explore the responsibility of chaplains in an institution. The function of chaplain has not changed much throughout the last ten years. The role can be simplified by two primary tasks:

1. The chaplain's primary task or role is one of custodian. Yes, he/she is a custodian to the altar of God. As a custodian over the chapel, he conveys the importance of the "house of God," even if it is just a converted assembly room in which the believers meet. The Chaplain's role is the business of ritual, worship, alms giving, communion and baptisms. As one can see, the importance of a chaplain lies in his stewardship to "God's Altar" wherever it might be.

2. The chaplain's secondary task or responsibility lies in establishing loyalties and the ability to make friends. The creation of relationships is most critical before any counseling can take place. Good chaplains make it a point to establish a trusting relationship that will cultivate an environment that is open for prayer, counsel and in some cases, life-changing counsel.

On a daily basis, the prison chaplain has the unique opportunity to touch the lives of so many suffering people. A day in the life of a prison chaplain can range from a quiet office day to a hectic fast-pace day of crisis counseling. However, in most cases, the chaplain fills his day coordinating religious services and developing counseling services to meet all the needs of both staff and inmates. Overall, the duties of a chaplain are:

- Offering sacramental ministries
- Coordinating ministries and other faith groups
- Liaisoning with administration
- Providing pastoral care counseling
- Counseling of inmates' families
- Serving as a pastor, guide and counselor to all in the facility
- Community liaisoning

- Maintaining the Altar of God, — the chapel. Although this is the most unglamorous task, it is the most important; it conveys a worth to the "Things of God" and dignifies God.

In most institutions today, the chaplains tend to be those individuals who have had no great clarification where they belong in both the realm of religion and in the secular world. This lack of identity often draws men and women into the chaplaincy. Because of the varying settings of a prison or a hospital, a mere knowledge of the Bible is not enough. The effective chaplain must have a calling (vocation) and academic training (i.e., at least a masters in theology or psychology) which entails the following course work:

○   Human Development

○   Theories of personality

○   Grief and loss

○   Cognitive therapy

○   Psychology of religion

○   Theories of addiction

○   Course work in victimology

Unfortunately, due to the inordinate cost of a graduate education, I truly believe the institution should help finance this education in exchange for a lengthy tenure.

With the passage of the Religious Freedom and Restoration Act, the prison chaplain should be a paramount figure in the correctional setting. However, in reality, he is not. In most institutions, the chaplain is under-utilized and in some cases rarely called upon.

Because of the ambiguity of the chaplain's role, few administrators find any reason to embrace the chaplain. Therefore, the chaplain is hardly called upon for crisis negotiation, referral or other critical situations. Due to this type of identity, the effective chaplains will learn to be autonomous and self-motivated in order to find a way to avail themselves. The key element to become an effective chaplain tends to be two-fold: An acute understanding of human nature to be able to relate to a broad range of people to increase his availability and the ability to integrate psychology with theology counseling to interact within the confines of the prison environment.

Like all fields, the chaplaincy has some "bad apples." All too often, many chaplains are aberrations – goofs that could not make it in the church world where success is based upon submission and the ability to get along with others. Hence, many find a niche in an institution where they perpetuate lives of ambiguity and mediocrity. In short, with a prison population that suffers from training, mental illness and addiction, it only makes sense to provide chaplains an opportunity to better themselves. The chaplaincy is an avocation of the most worthy cause and the minister who embraces the title of chaplain must commit to a life long process of education. THE INSTITUTION DESERVES IT!

We have witnessed over the past fifteen years the norm in most institutions appears to be "odd ball" ministers who find a spot in an institution where they can enjoy the privilege of honorifics and ego gratification. This commentary is sad, given the rich opportunity a prison offers for life-changing ministry opportunities. In this work we endeavor to continue to stress the value chaplains bring in the process of restoration. It is evident the therapeutic communities do not alone have all the answers or solutions for the prison inmate. But working together with solid chaplains is a pragmatic and brave attempt to provide the educational and spiritual benefits to these fellow human beings in crisis.

Chapter IX

The Therapeutic Communities

The therapeutic treatment approach to drug treatment is a sophisticated, psychological approach to treatment that has been long praised and criticized.

The raves and praises generally come from the Society of Clinical Psychologists, which is exactly where the nervous concerns come from.

As an accepted and challenging teaching curriculum, it has survived the criticism and is now being taught with success (e.g., reduction in recidivism) at the California Rehabilitation Center in Norco, CA.

The therapeutic treatment approach to drug treatment is a sophisticated, psychological approach to treatment that has been long praised and criticized.

The praises generally come from the Society of Clinical Psychologists, which is exactly where the criticism and nervous concerns come from.

As an accepted and challenging teaching curriculum, it has survived the criticism and is now being taught at the California Rehabilitation Center in Norco, California, a 5000 inmate facility, and in other selected major prisons in the United States.

The authors of this book feel the TC's, as they are known to the inmates, bring excellent training and information to the affected prison population. The discipline is strict and the knowledge shared is compelling. It has a theory, model and method of its own.[6]

The Therapeutic Communities

by George De Leon, Ph.D.

Invisible Boundaries

---

[6] George De Leon, PhD., "The Therapeutic Community."

The Physical Environment

Therapeutic communities (TCs) are designed, both physically and programmatically, to enhance the residents' experience of community within the residence. It is this experience of community—with all its features of safety, consistency, predictability, etc.—that gradually enables newcomers to lesson their identification with and ties to the old drug culture and replace them with ties and loyalties to the people, values, and lifestyle of the TC. This chapter explores how the physical environment of the TC, its setting, facilities, and inner environment, can contribute to this perception and affiliation with community.

SETTING, RESOURCES, AND THE TC PERSPECTIVE

TCs for the treatment of addiction are located in a variety of settings, which may be determined by funding sources and the external resistance to or acceptance of rehabilitaion programs. Some are situated on the attractive grounds of former camps, resorts, and ranches in rural settings, or in conventional houses or mansions in suburban neighborhoods. The majority, however, are located in inner-city areas often near drug-affected urban neighborhoods. These TCs are usually operated in building spaces converted from tenement housing, hotels, schools, churches, or nursing homes with the work of renovation frequently done with the assistance of program residents themselves. Larger, well-financed agencies may occupy several facilities in different settings to meet various clinical and administrative needs.

Invisible Boundaries

TCs seek to maintain a *social and psychological separateness* from the settings in which they are located. In the TC perspective on recovery, it is essential to remove the addict from the physical, social, and psychological surroundings previously associated with his or her loss of control and dysfunctional, negative lifestyle.

A complete chemical and "behavioral detoxification" is a necessary initial step in recovery. Residents must not only withdraw from the psychopharmacological effects of drug use, but must also detach from the people, places, and things previously associated with their drug use. This behavioral detox can be undermined if a new resident is constantly exposed to the world outside the TC, as he or she doesn't yet have the skills to resist the myriad of cues and triggers there. Indeed, the inability to maintain abstinence while living in the "real world" is usually the new resident's main reason for having to enter a residential program in the first place.

Secondly, drug subcultures are strong competitors to the positive peer culture of the TC. Thus separation from the outside world is needed to facilitate a gradual affiliation of the new resident with the TC community—a process essential to the TC approach.

Physical and psychological separation from the surrounding social setting is best achieved when the TC facility itself is located in a completely different area, such as a rural setting or even a city neighborhood relatively clear of drugs. However, residents must also learn how to cope with the "culture shock" when they return to the real world outside of the TC. Thus programs must achieve balance between separation from and preparation for re-entry into the outside world.

[25] Seperate re-entry facitlities are usually similar in design and concept to the program's main, primary residence, but smaller in size and capacity because they are expected to house fewer residents. There is also typically more private sleeping quarters, reflecting the greater autonomy afforded those in re-entry.

Some TC agencies operate multiple facilities so that those early in recovery can be initially housed far from their former negative influences but later transferred to a re-entry facility located in their home city or area. This gives them both the chance to solidify early recovery away from temptations and triggers *and* the chance to learn gradually how to cope with real-world influences during re-entry, before they become independently launched.[25]

Regardless of where the program is located, physical and psychological separateness is necessary to counter the negative influences of the outside world. Indeed, by assismilating residents into its own *inner* community, the program creates a new peer culture, new lifestyle, and new values to replace the old, destructive ones.

Relationship to the Larger Community

While striving to maintain their "invisible boundaries," TCs must, for both clinical and political reasons, simultaneously maintain good relations and a sense of being integrated with the larger community. Local communities often resist placement of TCs in their locale out of fear about having certain racial groups, criminals, and drug addicts in close proximity and the imagined effects on quality of life, real estate prices, etc. This "NIMBY" (not in my back yard) resistance can impede the implementation of new programs, often in areas where they are needed most. However, in actual experience, once programs are established, community perceptions usually reverse as people see and experience their new neighbors (the program) as responsible concerning upkeep, appearances, safety, and civic participation (Nash, 1974; Wexler, H., personal communication, July, 1999).

For example, TCs are vigilant in maintaining an impeccable physical and social image. They strive to have their facilities seen as exemplary homes by the larger community. Hence the physical condition of the facility and its external grounds are in constant attendance by residents. Even in inner-city settings, TCs are often perceived with pride by the local community, who may note that streets with TC facilities are the safest and cleanest in the neighborhood.

In terms of civic duty, teams of residents may be sent out to provide a variety of community services, such as cleaning local parks and assisting the elderly. Special presentations to schools, business groups, religious organizations, and civic groups may be provided by the facility at little or no cost. Other elements of TC life that often impress local residents are the exemplary behavior of residents in public places, the open house invitations, and the generally active and positive relations with various community boards. In fact, TCs usually have a community relations department dedicated specifically to promoting positive community perceptions concerning the health, safety, and social standards of the program.

Although maintaining good community relations is driven partly by political necessity, it also complements the TC's treatment goals. In a sense, the TC itself becomes a role model for good citizenry. Residents learn the value of maintaining good appearances and experience the positive regard that results. They learn to participate in the larger community in a responsible manner—something they've often never experienced before.

Resources

Most programs are primarily supported by public funding and must supplement their funding by seeking additional private and public donations. Thus, there is a wide variation in the amount of resources—financial and material—which agencies have at their disposal. Some own the buildings is which they operate; others lease space. Some are furnished entirely with donations of used articles from the community; others are beautifully furnished with new gear.

Whatever their basic level of public support, however, TCs typically incorporate fund-raising into their self-help approach, involving residents in these efforts as much as possible. For example, TCs routinely operate a "procurement department," which seeks from individuals and businesses in the larger community donations of everything from furnishings and clothing to sports equipment and electronics. Even foodstuffs, staples, and housewares are sometimes obtained at discounts negotiated with suppliers.

Residents may be involved in these procurement efforts through a work assignment. The procurement department operates under staff guidance and utilizes residents to serve on crews for street fund-raising campaigns, pick-up and delivery of donated goods, operation of the supply house, telephone negotiations with prospective donors, etc. In these roles, residents are like family members whose personal efforts to sustain the community also strengthen their affiliation *with* the community.

In addition, all residents in a TC must assume some responsibility for paying their own way. The large majority of residents in the typical TC are indigent and therefore unable to pay a fee. However, if they receive public assistance or food stamps, these allowances are donated to the program. Meanwhile, though their numbers are small, some residents with access to income are asked to pay a fee for their drug treatment. In the initial orientation, all new residents are made aware of the practical needs of the program and are helped to ascertain how they will contribute.

In the TC perspective the physical condition and resources of a TC facility convey important psychological messages to its residents. A building in disrepair, shabbily furnished, or serving poor-quality food can signal to residents that they are second-class citizens and reinforce their characteristically low self-esteem. Conversely, TCs housed in well-maintained, cheerful facilities providing appealing, well-prepared food convey the message "We value you and we expect you to value yourself. You deserve to live in nice surroundings." Even when TCs are located in poor neighborhoods, have more modest material resources, lack sufficient space, or have older furnishings, residents still learn the value of living with dignity if these modest accommodations are well-maintained.

While TCs stress the importance of maintaining decent living quarters, they also place this responsibility with the residents, as well as the staff. Giving the residents the job of maintaining and caring for the facility teaches them in a very concrete way. TCs are often the first attractive, orderly, and comfortable residences that many socially disadvantaged addicts have ever lived in. Living in such surroundings helps to reinforce a shift in identity and higher expectations for themselves. "I *can* live in someplace nice, and I can keep it up. I want to keep doing this in the future." Learning to care for the facility provides a corrective learning experience that often contrasts with early experiences of deprivation, low expectations, and disorder. Even residents from advantaged backgrounds, who are accustomed to material benefits, often have never experienced the sense of earning these.

Notwithstanding the differences in the socioeconomic status of its residents, the TC utilizes its setting and resources to teach residents distinctions between inner *psychological* and outer *physical* space. This involves learning attitudes and values that are consistent with recovery and right living. Residents are taught to care for their living space and its furnishings; but in addition, they learn to value personal growth more than material gain, to cope with rather than escape the limitations of the "real" world, and to make the best of their existing reality while actively working to change it.

THE FACILITY

The physical characteristics of a given TC—its size, grounds, condition, and inner spaces—are adapted to the TC's aims and teachings in various ways. Although each TC is laid out differently, there are common physical features that can be identified and their rationale explored through the TC perspective.

Size and Capacity

The residential capacity of a TC program varies widely ranging from 30 in small agencies to 2000 in large agencies that administer separate programs housed in multiple residential facilities. Typically, however, a particular "house" in a community-based setting will accommodate 40-80 residents.

Some houses are surrounded by expansive grounds, such as the land around a former farm, ranch, or resort. Others have only the lot that accompanies a suburban home, or, in the case of an urban tenement building, a small rear courtyard. The external space has programmatic and management implications for the TC.

For example, large open spaces are alluring to residents prone to "wander off" physically or psychologically, particularly early in treatment when least committed to the long-term recovery process. Even for more stable residents, the hidden corners and remote areas of sprawling grounds invite behaviors that are proscribed by the community, such as drug use, sexual acting out, or social withdrawal. Although these security issues are present in all TCs on large campuses, special procedures may be required to monitor residents.

For these reasons, modest-sized facilities and grounds are generally more easily managed and have other important benefits as well: The experience of family and community is more easily shaped and strengthened when people are living and working within close proximity to each other; and, the compression of limited space intensifies the 24-hour living and learning process, as it evokes a wide range of emotions and attitudes that cannot be easily masked nor escaped by physically isolating oneself.

The "static capacity" of a TC is the maximum number of residents it can house at any one time. For instance, a TC may be a "40-bed" facility or can maintain "40 slots." Clinical and managerial experience has shown that a static capacity of between 40 and 80 is optimal. A critical mass of residents (about 40) is necessary for shaping the stratified peer structure (e.g., junior, intermediate, and senior residents) and filling all the posts needed in the hierarchical division of labor. This allows for vertical mobility, variations in status, and defined role models—elements considered essential to the TC model. Also, with at least 40 residents, goods can be purchased with economy of scale. More than 80 becomes cumbersome in terms of supervision and can work against building a cohesive sense of community.[26]

The "dynamic capacity" is the *actual* number of admissions per year. This is usually about four times higher than the static capacity. Given client turnover—through completion or graduation, client dropout, administrative discharge, etc.—the program may service many more than "40 beds" over the course of the year (for a full discussion of retention rates see De Leon, 1991; De Leon & Schwartz, 1984; Sells & Simpson, 1976).

Access

Residential TCs are not locked facilities but semi-closed environments with restricted access. Doors are generally locked only at night; however, while a resident is in primary treatment (approximately 12 months), the program imposes strict limitations on his or her comings and goings. A resident's whereabouts is monitored with sign-in and sign-out sheets

---

[26] In recent years, some larger agencies operate residential facilities with a static capacity of 200-300 in community-based settings even larger numbers in prison settings. Formative evaluations suggest that these capacities are feasible if managed as smaller units of 50-100 residents (e.g., Corcoran prison in California). Conversly, modified TC programs in shelters and mental health settings are smaller "houses" of 30-50 residents (e.g., De Leon, 1997a; Liberty et al., 1998). Increasingly, issues such as resident capacity, staff to client ratios, and number of programming hours are under regulatory influences (e.g. California Department of Corrections, 1998).

and bulletin boards. Trips to the outside include legal or medical appointments or family obligations (funerals, organized recreational or other special events attended outside the facility, etc., all of which are usually escorted). Residents may also perform special job-related assignments for the agency such as purchasing or driving vehicles.

Increased access is a privilege granted to residents showing clinical improvement over time. As residents demonstrate greater personal responsibility and appear more prepared to safely engage the outside world, they will be given more frequent and wider access to it. These are provided through day and overnight passes and weekend furloughs. During the re-entry phase of treatment, residents may also be allowed to attend work or an educational/ training program. The rationale for limiting resident access to the outside world is the same as that discussed earlier regarding TC settings. There is a need to separate residents from the outside world in order to strengthen their sense of community and affiliation and also to reduce the number of negative pulls from the outside world that could threaten recovery. However, because the doors of a TC are not literally locked, a resident technically *chooses* to stay in the program each day, and this sense of personal choice helps to reinforce affiliation with the community.

Security

Residents themselves, under staff supervision, manage security. The main security tasks are to restrict unauthorized entry into and exit from the facility and to monitor the movements of residents around the grounds. One work assignment involves operating the "front desk," typically located near the main entrance. There, residents maintain daily logs of all access events, greet and sign visitors in, and handle all phone calls. In large facilities, additional residents may be stationed at critical junctures, such as the entrance to floors, corridors, and rooms not authorized for general use, to record activity and report incidents.

Unlike institutions such as jails, hospitals, or schools, TCs do not generally hire any police or guards to oversee security, instead relying on the residents themselves with staff supervision. This is a striking fact considering the profile of residents and the nature of the substance abuse disorder. Significant numbers of residents and staff have histories of arrest and incarceration; they have typically engaged in crimes against property and sometimes people, while prominent features of their personalities are low frustration tolerance and poor impulse control. These characteristics would challenge the security of any setting.

Resident management of security is a central tenet of the TC perspective and approach. The physical safety of the community is maximized when residents are empowered to hold themselves accountable.

THE INNER ENVIRONMENT

Spaces, rooms, and areas characterize the features of the TC inner environment. These may be ordinary in every way, but are utilized to reinforce, again, the experience of community, the fostering of a sense of home and ownership, the assurance of physical and psychological safety, and a setting that is conducive to personal interaction. All of these goals are inherent in the TC perspectives on recovery and right living.

Space and Area

The key spaces in a TC are where the operational, educational, and therapeutic activities of the program are held. A few TCs, such as those located on ranches and farms, consist of complexes of single-story buildings, some used for sleeping dorms, others for administration, etc., all organized around a main house in which all of the communal activities occur. Most often, though, the TC facility is a single, self-contained, multi-level building that consists of a kitchen, dining room, sleeping quarters, administrative offices, and group and recreational rooms.

Although TCs vary in physical layout, they all attempt to utilize their space to best facilitate communal functions. Because of their typically modest resources, limited space must be creatively converted to serve multiple purposes. For instance, an area might serve as a group room by day, a seminar room in the evening, and a living room for a party on the weekend. With some exceptions, most common areas are also available at various times for contemplation, social interaction, one-on-one conversations, and spontaneous rap groups. The dining room is the area most often converted for other activities such as parties, dances, general meetings, and large seminars.

The rooms of the TC can be organized into common, private, and specially designated areas. Common spaces consist of lounges, the dining room, sitting areas, classrooms, the library, recreational areas, and resident dormitories. Private spaces (out of bounds without permission) are the offices and conference room used by staff and the residents assigned there for work. Specially designated spaces include those used for specific purposes, such as the kitchen, bathrooms, laundry room, group rooms, relating booths (areas set aside for one-on-one conversations), and the "bench" (an area set aside for self-examination).

The *kitchen* in a TC is customarily large and equipped for institutional cooking. This is not common space, but space in which only authorized residents belong. One staff person supervises it with a senior resident and a changing work crew of other residents. Labor is divided to handle the ordering and purchasing of food, meal planning, food storage and preparation, cooking, maintenance of the area and equipment, and kitchen cleanup. The work activity in the kitchen and dining room is ongoing from early morning until after dinner. Smaller programs often have small eating areas adjacent to the kitchen for off-hour snacks and socializing. Larger programs have snacks served in the dining room or sold in commissaries operated by residents.

The *dining room* is usually one of the largest areas in the facility. Managed by a senior resident, a crew of residents is responsible for setting up the room for three meals a day and snacks. Tasks include arrangement of chairs and tables, table setting, meal service, and dining room cleanup. In the practical sense, residents learn to set place settings, wait on tables, serve meals, bus tables. As in the kitchen, working in the dining room also gives residents the opportunity to provide hands-on service to the community.

Communal meals are a time when most staff and peer level groups—senior, junior, and new admissions—come together for 30-45 minutes, three times a day. This is a distinctive example of how the TC uses community as method. Communal meals provide an opportunity for learning the conventions of social manners, dinning, conversation, and appropriate interpersonal behavior—all of which are typically modeled by senior residents. Residents learn how to say "please" and "thank you" respectfully, to speak in moderate tones, and to display respect for the food served and for those who prepared and served it.

It is not uncommon for intense personal and social discussions to transpire around the dining table as residents learn the art of conversation and social discourse. Various social anxieties may surface during mealtime. By having to relate to others in close physical proximity—like a "normal family"—residents learn to sit and talk with people they may not particularly like, to speak about ordinary subjects like the news or weather, and even discuss personal issues related to their experiences in the program. Were they not in this treatment situation, the same residents might characteristically react to such a communal situation with hostility, withdrawal, early departure, or by sitting alone or with cliques of familiar others for "social protection."

Dining room behaviors and attitudes may be the material for encounter groups but more often are addressed in informal peer conversation. Senior peers serve both as role models for healthy dining room behavior and as supporters and trainers. They may actively "pull-in" (orient and engage) new residents with invitations and suggestions, such as "Come, let's eat together and tell me how you're doing," or "Why don't you sit here with us and talk to the women," or "Make sure you sit with different people every day."

Lounges are separate areas set aside for informal interactions, individual relaxation and reading, TV watching, listening to music, or simply sitting quietly. TC lounges and day rooms are typically carpeted and furnished with sofas, a variety of upholstered and hard chairs, reading lamps and material, and wall hangings.

In many TCs, the evening news is played in the lounge after dinner, with residents required or encouraged to watch and become informed about the world around them. The newscast can stimulate discussion, comments, and controversy, usually initiated by a senior resident or staff member. Residents are encouraged to freely offer opinions, ideas, and suggestions about a variety of social issues. Thus, the evening newscast becomes another "family"—like ritual fostering communication, intellectual expression, and community interaction on issues outside the TC and beyond the usual focus on individual growth. For a staff member observing such a discussion, the level of participation and the quality of the exchanges can also be of clinical utility in gauging the level of affiliation or general progress of the residents involved.

Although largely informal and spontaneous, the activities in the lounge can reveal much about the social and psychological status of individuals—and indeed the house in general. The lounge is only available for use to residents during certain hours of the day, e.g., during personal time after dinner, before evening house meetings, after evening groups, and on weekends. Thus, a lounge with too many residents at any one point is a negative sign in a TC. In the lounge, where there are fewer program demands, the social manners, attitudes, and energy level of individuals are often revealed. Hence, all members of the community are expected to observe the behavior and tone of the lounge. Behaviors such as avoiding others, bullying, yelling, sleeping, or forming small exclusionary groups are indicators of socialization and affiliation problems.

In larger TCs, there may be adequate space to set aside permanent rooms for classes, seminars, and workshops. *Classrooms* will typically be furnished with desks, chairs, lecterns, blackboards, flipcharts, overhead and 35 mm. projectors and screens, and computers. Separate areas may be designated for vocational training in carpenty/woodworking, printing, auto repair, etc. In those TCs that are smaller and have fewer resources, however, there may be no permanent schoolroom and so other common space will be converted as needed.

Whatever the degree of furnishings, when a room is being used as a classroom, the residents there are expected to behave as students. Emphasis is upon proper sitting, paying attention, taking notes, speaking, listening, and observing the rules of the classroom. Sleeping, dozing, speaking out of turn, or displays of temper or disrespect are considered negative behaviors that will be noted by senior peers and staff.

There are special spaces in the facility dedicated to encourage social relating. For example, a table and chairs arranged in a corner or hallway may be designated as a *relating area* or *relating booth.* These special areas afford space for prescribed social interaction, where residents can practice and rehearse relating to each other, person to person. Residents are expected to use these areas for one-on-one conversations that focus on shared experiences and immediate problem solving, as distinguished from confrontation or instruction. For example, staff may suggest that two junior residents talk to each other about whatever feelings they have about adjusting to the program; or, a male and female resident may talk to each other about their perceptions of each other. Although removed enough to promote private conversations, the relating areas are in full view of the passing community, so that peers and staff can observe the activity and participants involved.

Another designated relating area is a chair or bench placed near the front door of the facility. Referred to as "the bench," it provides a place for an individual to sit alone and think about matters that may be disturbing or provocative. For residents experiencing great hostility or upset, the bench provides a place to go for "time out" in order to cool down. Often the bench is used for residents who are threatening to drop out of the program. It permits them the opportunity to emotionally settle down, review the circumstances precipitating their wanting to leave, and evaluate the "pros" and "cons" of doing so—all in close proximity of the exit door. Although alone on the bench, the resident observes the familiar faces of peers who remain in the daily struggle for recovery and, conversely, peers witness and silently encourage the individual in his or her crisis period or period of decision. Though not readily obvious, these social factors indirectly contribute to residents' assessments concerning their status and future.

The relating booth and bench are examples of how the TC physical environment is designed to foster certain behaviors, attitudes and values. Spaces are designated and used variously to foster social and individual relating, interrupt impulsive behavior, and provide opportunities to reflect. In all of these uses of space, the community is indirectly utilized to help monitor, support, and encourage "right living." So while the designated areas are used for semiprivate activity, they are of public importance to the entire community.

Sleeping quarters

Sleeping quarters reflect the hierarchical structure of the program. Quarters are arranged by seniority status, ranging from 2-4 bed dormitories to semi-private and private rooms. The dorm rooms—however modestly furnished are required to be kept clean and orderly. A standard TC teaching, "clean bed, clean head," highlights the psychological importance of maintaining an orderly and clean personal living space, regardless of the quarters.

All dorms are segregated by gender, often with female and male sleeping areas located on separate floors or wings of the facility to facilitate management and security. In the TC perspective, it is noted that residents characteristically have had past difficulties with sexual acting out, and many have histories of sexual abuse, street or exploitative sexuality, low tolerance for sexual restraint, and a tendency toward sexual impulsivity. Moreover, the physical and social intimacy of communal life in the TC can intensify even healthy sexuality.

Considerable effort is put into helping residents resolve such histories of sexual disturbance and teaching them healthy sexual attitudes, values, and practices. Central to this effort is a requirement that while in residential treatment, all residents restrain from all forms of sexual contact with anyone in the program or outside. An exception to this is accorded some residents during the later stages of the program, when permission may be granted to engage in sage sex while on furlough.

Resident dormitories may also be separated by age. In age-integrated TCs the adolescents (residents under 18 years of age) are housed on separate floors or in separate facilities. (In TCs that treat adolescents exclusively sleeping quarters remain gender-segregated). Though separated by gender and age group, roommates may nonetheless be of differing racial and ethnic backgrounds. Communal life is utilized to explore and resolve issues of race-ethnic diversity and cultural sensitivities (e.g., De Leon, Melnick, Schoket, & Jainchill, 1993).

Residents' toilets and showers are also separated by gender. Separate bathrooms are generally provided for staff reflecting their distinction in the program hierarchy. A service crew is assigned to maintain bathrooms, including cleaning urinals and toilet bowls, replacing paper supplies, etc. In the hierarchy of jobs, these chores are generally assigned to new admissions. As sleeping quarters, residents are instructed to spend only necessary time in toilets and bathrooms, and frequent room and floor-checks by staff and resident monitors assure that peers are not tarrying there. As active addicts, bathrooms and bedrooms were often places where residents went to use drugs or alcohol, avoid obligations, or socially withdraw; they are, therefore, associated with avoidance, negative, and unproductive thinking and behavior.

Privacy

Practically all individuals and collective activities in the TC are convened in public spaces, reflecting the TC's perspective and method. Living and working in an open community helps to (a) discourage personal isolation and withdrawal into the self, (b) promote peer solidarity and affiliation through interpersonal relating, (c) foster cooperative "teamwork" through group management of communal and personal spaces, and (d) encourage accountability through the constant observation of the individual by the community.

Individual privacy is highly valued, but within the context of the TC perspective, privacy is considered an earned privilege based on the individual's social and psychological growth. Private time and space are gradually increased in direct proportion to a resident's successful self-management, acceptance of increasing responsibility, role model attributes, and proven accountability to the community. For example, residents afforded more privacy are those who have demonstrated the ability to constructively manage time alone, successfully counter negative thoughts, participate fully in work and program activities, exhibit appropriate social manners, and make good decisions on furlough when coping with potential relapse traps, triggers, and cues.

Residents move into a TC with only the necessities (change of clothing, toothbrush, underwear). The first tangible symbol of earned privacy is being assigned to a small dormitory of semiprivate room. At certain stages of the program, residents may furnish these with personal accessories, such as a radio or CD player purchased from their own earnings or savings or received as gifts. How these spaces are furnished and decorated also reflects the individual's development and growth. Photographs, quotes, posters, or slogans on the walls conveying positive messages about right living signify more maturity and responsibility than, for example, pinups or commercial posters of consumer products.

HALLMARK FEATURES OF THE TC

There are four physical features of the inner environment that instantly identify what is unique about a TC program: the front desk, the structure board, wall signs, and decorative artifacts. However mundane, these features sustain the perception of community in both functional and symbolic ways.

The Front Desk

All traffic in and out of the TC is monitored at a desk situated close to the main entrance of the facility. Residents who are alert, cordial, and neatly dressed answer the telephones, handle the mail, and greet, screen, and direct all visitors. Under staff supervision they maintain a 24-hour watch, recording on a daily sign-in log the names of all visitors, their times of arrival and departure, and their destinations within the facility.

Working at the front desk is a highly valued, earned position, which like other job functions has educational and therapeutic elements. It trains residents in useful skills that are relevant to almost any kind of future work. The requirements and responsibilities of the position inherently strengthen the resident's sense of ownership and affiliation with the program. Front desk residents are the first to be seen by outsiders as well as new client admissions, and hence are the front-line representatives of the program to the outside world. Maturity, responsibility, efficiency, and an appropriate business demeanor are all needed to work the front desk. To the visitor, the residents at the front desk convey self-management in action, a sense of order in the facility, and optimism about the potential of recovery.

Structure Boards and Other Charts

On the walls behind or near the front desk is typically a large rectangular corkboard or blackboard that displays the structure of the TC in terms of its staff, key operational activities, and current functioning. This organizational chart visually reflects the stratification of the entire facility's membership, their identities, community position or program phase status, and where they are on a daily basis. Typically, it lists the names and positions of staff, peer level of residents (junior, intermediate, and senior) or their program phase (induction/

orientation, primary, early, re-entry, live-out, etc.), and their job or work crew function (kitchen, maintenance, etc.).

Additional charts may display monthly, weekly, and daily schedules of planned activities; a daily update of the population, house counts, scheduled trips, and appointments (legal, medical, etc.); those on furlough; the names of new admissions; and recent dropouts. Still another chart may picture the personnel and positions within the entire TC agency similar to organizational charts in conventional business settings.

Structure boards are explicitly used as general visual aides for the daily management and operation of the facility. However, their implicit use is to strengthen residents' perception of community and their affiliation with the program. For example, the listing of names facilitates recognition of the people in the community; the daily schedule and activities charts disseminate up-to-the-hour information about community members; the daily schedule board helps the resident set boundaries and give direction to the day; and the stratification of status and location helps the resident place himself within the community.

The various structure boards and charts provide a snapshot of the facility at any one time. But over time, they also provide a visual picture of mobility within the program by showing who has moved up and to where they've moved (a new job, in or out of the facility), thereby illustrating clear paths of navigation through the program.

Wall Signs

Whereas structure boards display concrete data about the organization of the program and its inhabitants, signs posted throughout the facility reinforce the philosophical basis for the community. Signs—often simple in form but profound in meaning—hang on the walls in practically all spaces and areas of a TC and are another essential element of the therapeutic environment. In words, phrases, slogans, and occasionally in pictures, the messages of recovery and right living stand as ever-present visual reminders of the TC's teachings and provide silent, continuous reinforcement to the residents.

The general function of these signs is to raise and maintain awareness of the TC teachings. Some specific themes often expressed in signs are encouragement ("every day in every way"), caution ("guilt kills") and coping strategies ("one day at a time"), or hope and equanimity (the AA Serenity Prayer). Usually written in the casual, colloquial language reflecting the real world of the substance user, signs variously employ metaphor, concrete advice, and symbolism. They may be a simple drawing or painting on paper, or an artful wood engraving.

Generally, signs reiterate the basic and relevant themes running through treatment. The phrases on the signs are often the same words spoken in groups and in peer conversations. They provide something for the individual to reflect on as he or she moves about the facility. They are ever-present reminders of what is needed or useful for recovery and personal growth.

Many of the same signs appearing in the variety of contemporary TCs were also in early programs, illustrating how the TC culture has been transmitted across the generations irrespective of geography. They also reflect the expression of common, if not universal, experiences associated with recovery in self-help communities.

Historically, TC residents initiated the use of signs themselves. Many TC signs are now considered traditional, developed by earlier generations of residents and bequeathed to the program. However, signs are continually being reinvented, designed by successive generations and added to the treasury. Indeed, the making of signs is viewed as an instructional and therapeutic activity in its own right; a resident may be asked, for example, to make a particular sign in order to reinforce that specific concept in himself or herself.

The program philosophy is usually the largest, most elaborate sign hanging in a TC. Typically, it was created and written by one or more of the initial founding cadre of residents. The philosophy distinguishes the unique character and culture of each TC. It instantly becomes traditional, signifying its powerful role in the recovery of past generations of residents and holding forth hope to future generations. Daily reciting of the philosophy in the morning keeps it alive in the community, while memorizing it is an explicit measure of program affiliation.

Decorative artifacts

All TCs purposely seek to transform their inner environments into home-like surroundings regardless of setting. The artwork, poetry, sculpture, and crafts often created by residents are typically displayed in suitable places. In fact, the cheerfulness of the TC inner environment may be in stark contrast to the impersonal treatment environments found in conventional clinic or residential settings, especially within institutions such as prisons or psychiatric hospitals.

The artifacts displayed not only help to define the culture of that specific TC, but promote self-expression, self-esteem, and affiliation. Common among decorations are photographs of staff, graduating classes, and founding residents or "pioneers." These smiling faces transmit optimism and the possibility of change, while promoting identification with similar—albeit unknown—others who have lived the same struggle to overcome addiction and change lifestyles. The artifacts mirror the people, perspective, and culture of the TC.

CONCLUSION

This chapter has described how the physical environment of a TC facility is designed to foster a culture of change. Its separateness from the outside community in addition to its living spaces, furnishings, and décor are all utilized to promote affiliation, a sense of order, safety, and right living. Within this inner environment is a social and psychological ecology—the structure, people, and activities that define the TC as a treatment model.

Chapter X

The Academic Expansion Versus Brick, Mortar and Fences

When I drove up the highway to the prison, I saw a sea of brown and black faces exercising in the prison yard. It was then I realized there is something strangely wrong with our society.

Eddie Olivas III

X

Experienced chaplains and parole officers working with parolees, develop an acute sense of what works and what does not. An astute onlooker working in skid row (in downtown Los Angeles) can see a permanent underclass developing. This emerging population strangely reflects the state's prison system. The men who live on skid row either live in tents or slum apartments. The common reality is that these men are all on parole! The streets of skid row reflect a crisis – a breakdown of family, our public schools and our prisons. Presently, an onlooker driving through downtown would see hundreds of minority men drinking, sleeping and smoking crack in open view. The sight is utterly shocking. This problem is pandemic (to a certain degree); however, it affects all in the area. Homeless, drug dependent parolees have deeply affected many shopkeepers, small manufacturers and the innocent working poor. Hence, I firmly think the CDC has some responsibility to address this perplexing problem. It is most obvious that the police in the downtown area concur with this view. – Chaplain Eddie Olivas, III

With 6.2 percent of the state budget going to California's correctional programs,[8] we must ask what is going on? Moreover, with the average yearly cost of $28,502 per prisoner and $2,882 per parole, we must ask: What the taxpayer is receiving for his/her hard-earned dollars? This perplexing social malady will not go away until the people of California start raising these hard questions to their leaders of the CDC. If we fail to address the way the prison system operates, we will truly regret the outcome. With approximately 1,700 homeless parolees in the Los Angeles area, one can see the numbers are not going down.

[8] California Fiscal Budget, 2002 – 2003.

With a dramatic growing parolee population, the only people benefiting appear to be the employees of the CDC, mainly due to job stability.

"The CDC is like a giant machine; an engine that runs best on a high octane fuel: men of color…" – an anonymous parolee

In the following account lies some startling truth in that on any given day, in the prison system, there are an alarming number of Black and Hispanic men in the system according to the second quarter CDC report. Based on these numbers, Blacks and Hispanics comprise over 65 percent of the prison population. This reality should not be alarming given the American public's tendency to couple crime with minorities.

There are a lot of well-meaning people working in the system, however, the current philosophy and the "old way" of doing business still prevails. Much needs to be done to move the system away from its punitive doctrine, which has proven to be ineffective and is now adversely affecting the many communities into which nearly 37,000 parolees have been dispersed in Los Angeles County alone. This growing new underclass is becoming a new social dynamic.

There are no quick fixes, no one solution or no one course of acting that will fix this perplexing problem. Nevertheless, we must start with what we know works. In every modern civilization what works in dealing with addiction and anti-social behavior is coercion and knowledge. In treating addiction there are two primary factors – motivation to change and the information to initiate and sustain change.

"At 58 years old, I spent 38 years of my life in prison or robbing and shooting dope. I thought this was how to live. I accepted this lifestyle until someone gave me some information in prison...it was then I began to change my perspective on my life and the world around me." Howard – a recovering addict

We are not advancing the precept that knowledge solves everything. Instead, we are simply stating that the "after prison" population has created new problems which need to be examined and addressed.

There is a systemic failure in the large California prison system. Expanding the prison industry by building more and more prisons in the empty desert is an expensive attempt to fix an education problem. It is not presently working and it holds no hope for the inmates or society in California's future. We are in a new millennium, which brings a new opportunity to offer more education, counseling and work opportunities to both the inmates housed in the system and to its parolees.

The Department of Corrections has the ability to usher in some of these changes, first by examining its Spartan philosophy regarding the "care and feeding" of its inmates to one that includes the desire to help those inmates who can be helped. This new attitude should discourage the archaic perception of warehousing inmates and look to newer ways to deal with the prison population.

Chapter XI

Why A New Approach Is Needed

Alcohol is legal, usually tastes good and when imbibed in moderation, can contribute to a temporary sense of aiding relaxation and combating stress.

Substance abuse, however, is a totally different story that can lead to damaging careers, relationships, self esteem and health. Even more, it can lead to prison, as can drug addiction, which is almost a guaranteed paradigm for a trip to prison.

XI

Alcohol is legal, usually tastes good and when imbibed in moderation can contribute to a temporary sense of aiding relaxation and combating stress. Substance abuse, however, is taking advantage of alcohol and can lead to damaging careers, relationships, self-esteem and health. Even more, it can lead to prison. Alcohol is considered to be the number one drug offender by substance abuse educators and counselors, doctors, and many law enforcement departments because of the following reasons:

- It is legal.

- It is generally inexpensive.

- It creates an aura of well being.

- Seemingly, it alleviates one's problems.

- Commercials, television and movies promote alcohol consumption as an acceptable social function and an essential of the "good life."

- Drinking is often viewed by men as being macho and by women as glamorous.

Drug addiction, on the other hand, is an entirely different sensory assault. Drug addiction is almost a guaranteed paradigm for a trip to prison.

- Drugs without prescription are illegal.

- Compared to alcohol, they are more expensive.

- Generally, their effects are short-lived and as the body builds up a resistance, it requires even larger dosages.

- Because of its illegality, the user comes into contact with criminal elements.

- Armed dealers, sometimes rip off buyers and otherwise take advantage of male and female users.

- Heavy addiction can be a very degrading and debilitating behavior flaw and like alcohol abuse, can lead to serious health problems or death.

- Even more so than alcohol abuse, drug abuse can cause crimes against property which often results in incarceration.

We have already discussed substance abuse in some detail as one of the root causes for many of our citizens (and some non-citizens) to become acquainted with our criminal justice system. Henceforth, we should look at all prisons as an opportunity to begin the rehabilitation process with serious alcohol and drug abusers. We again urge the expansion of credentialed teachers and counselors throughout California prisons. The solution to pollution is dissolution. No one should lead a life in a body that is being destroyed by toxic substance abuse. Remember, we are only talking about abuse here. Legally obtained prescribed drugs have saved more lives than any other option available for sick people. Alcohol, used in moderation can be okay for many people.

A professional, prescribed curriculum in the therapeutic communities facilitated and taught by specially trained educated teachers and counselors to a controlled audience with lots of time can work wonders. Again, incarceration without education is just doing time! An inmate properly prepared for parole will reduce recidivism and return our citizens to communities for productive happy lives. "No Child Should Be Left Behind" as President Bush has conveyed, and no inmate who is eligible for and desires to participate should be left behind for the lack of rehabilitative programs.

A few years ago, cars traversing on the California streets were emblazoned with bumper stickers which read, God Don't Make No Junk! An accomplished civil society should empower their prisons to "un-trash" these citizens who have admittedly trashed themselves. Through thoughtful and meaningful rehabilitation efforts, they can again become tax paying, productive citizens.

California prison management emphasis is far too full of yesterday. As we have previously stated, the prison unions have too much sway over prison management. In some instances, their role has been described as "Thugs" in possession of the keys to the prison. Oftentimes, in order to help the prisoners, the guards are required to alter their mentality to the level of the prisoners in order to attain their intimidated respect. However, once that is achieved, the difference that separates the prisoner and his guard should be a higher sense of humanity. The union leadership is often insolent and resort to power politics to maintain their grip over the system. All of the special interest groups should be governed by specific guidelines to ensure the interrelationship between that programs' impact on the overall prison population. When the special interest groups begin to pull together rather than for their own separate agendas, hopefully, a proper value system may evolve.

No, God doesn't produce any junk, and we should help prevent our brothers and sisters from further trashing themselves. And we should be able to do it for far less than it costs to build with more brick, mortar and fences.

TREATMENT WORKS!

Chapter XII

Conclusion

This book is not intended to be regarded as a panacea for prison reform or a footprint for exit programs for inmates who have successfully completed their mandated sentences.

Our hope is that the California prison system will become more enlightened and education-conscious in these thin budget years. The Department of Corrections needs to be on top of the special interests, particularly the unions, who have run amok within the system. It needs to seriously examine the Correctional Counseling program and train counselors to know what they are doing. Competently trained counselors can help cut recidivism by really reaching out to inmates with educational tools and solid background training concepts.

Proper assimilation back into society must become a priority for inmate release!

XII

This book is not intended to be regarded as a panacea for prison reform or a footprint for exit programs for inmates who have successfully completed their mandated sentences. Our hope is that the California prison system will become more enlightened and education-conscious in these thin budget years needed to retain its leadership role in America.

California has long been regarded as one of the most innovative places in the world. Though not desired nor a priority, the inmate prison journey need not be limited to detention and punishment. It should also be a positive learning experience that will help the prisoner to positively reassimilate back into society. Their personal value systems should be uplifted and challenged by knowledgeable instructors and counselors who know how to interact and facilitate treatment in the classroom or group setting.

Certainly a portion of the correctional prison budget allocated for additional expansion of the system could be redirected to include a first-class educational institution as a part of its current building program. Reducing recidivism should not continue to be a Pavlovian endeavor. Inmates exposed to a strong learning environment will be far less likely to return to criminality in that they will emerge from their confinement better equipped to cope upon their re-entry into society.

Workplace politics, competition, job ability, rivalry, varying educational levels and ethnic problems are intense among the prison workforce. Although these problems exist in almost every industry, they are more vexing because of the closed environment of the prisons and the sustained hierarchical relationship between the inmates, staff and the administration.

The staffs of most prisons are unionized. The unions have grown to a position of power which literally allows the prison workforce to be controlled by bargaining units contracts and agreements. Prison correctional officers are paid well due, in part, to the union representation which stresses the inmates contempt of authority and the potential eventual confrontation between the staff and the inmates. All state prison staffs are unionized and the union rules and regulations help to enforce a balanced workplace.

Because of their growing influence, the unions represent a powerful lobby force in the state capital. Support and campaign dollars are eagerly sought after by numerous politicians, many of whom are inclined to look favorably upon legislation and appointments sympathetic to the union's role in the prisons. This relationship, though sometimes contentious, often reenforces the brick, mortar and fences attitude, in that it invariably promotes more benefits for the staff and the appearance of security to the populace from the inmates. But what is missing from this mix is the reformation and the educational training programs needed to prepare the inmates for reassimilation into society.

The Beginning

Acknowledgements

The CRC GED program is a colossal success, as noted earlier in this book. However, as this book is written, vocational and academic programs have been cut at CRC and all other California prisons due to the state's recent fiscal restrictions and the cozy relationship existing between the unions and the prisons' administration. Everyone should be entitled to a livable wage which considers reasonable qualifications, hazards of the job, experience and ongoing training. Salaries and cost of living adjustments and perks are certainly important. But the prison operation needs an honest and cogent overview from a Department of Corrections that is on the top of its game. When a pack of wolves (e.g., the unions) run the chicken coops, feathers will fly and ulterior motives will prevail. The union movement is a needed and honorable dynamic in the prison system, but only if it is measured and responsible. When a "thug" mentality governs the pay and promotions of 1800 prison guards, all is not well at the prison.

It is our hope that this book will help point out some of the systemic needs and actions of a progressive prison plan that is wounded by a powerful union lobby and elected officials who desire to be reelected. Hopefully, this book can help create an atmosphere to bring about the changes necessary to let California prisons become the best in the nation in educating, training and counseling the inmates. The prison system should create an opportunity for the inmates to rehabilitate themselves with suitably equipped prison employees guiding and leading them toward that goal.

Sometimes incarceration is the only alternative left to attempt to restructure a wavering soul and broken life. Let us not miss this opportunity. We should lead. We should educate. We should rehabilitate.

Lastly, we should truly create and transform the prison system to be stern when necessary, but noted for its successful parolees who do not come back.

The author would like to take this opportunity to thank Warden Jo Ann Gorden and her Chief Deputy Warden Gerimena Hall for the privilege of working at the California Rehabilitation Center in Norco, California. We sincerely salute them on the many changes and progressive action they have taken at CRC in the establishment of Therapeutic Treatment Centers and a strong Substance Abuse Program for the men and women inmates; all taught and facilitated by credentialed staff. These inmates have certainly proven the theory that "Treatment Works" by lowering their rate of recidivism (reincarceration) after leaving CRC – the true barometer of measuring treatment programs anywhere.

Special thanks to Cypress College, in Cypress California and its Human Service Department for their excellent leadership and development of Certificate Programs in Alcohol and Drug Studies, Victimology and Criminal Justice which produces students able to understand and work in and with the prison profession. Thanks in particular to Dr. Cindy

Alibrandi, educator magnifique and Human Services Department head who has taught and directed the lives and thinking of thousands of students who continually apply the knowledge gained from her in their daily work.

Thank you to Chaplain Eddie Olivas, III for his work and contributions to chapters eight and ten of this book.

And a big hug and special thanks to Linda and Trish, our beloved wives and patient partners who have inspired and supported us to write this book. It possibly would not be as human without their thoughts and certainly not as positive and compassionate.

Bibliography

1. Inside Corrections, California Department of Corrections Communications office, March, 1994.

2. The O'Reilly Factor, Bill O'Reilly

3. The Urban Institute, Jeremy Travis, Senior Fellow, August, 2002

4. The Therapeutic Communities, The Model, Chapter X

5. All about the Civil Addict Program, prepared by Addict Evaluation Authority, CRC, P.O. Box 1841, Norco, CA, Revised April, 1994

6. California Code of Regulations, Title 15, Crime Prevention and Corrections. Updated through September 15, 1994

Appendix

Pelican Bay State Prison

High Desert State Prison
California Correctional Center

California Medical Facility
CSP Solano
CSP San Quentin

Folsom State Prison
CSP Sacramento (New Folsom)
Mule Creek State Prison
Northern California Women's Facility
Sierra Conservation Center

Deuel Vocational Institution

Valley State Prison For Women
Central California Women's Facility

Correctional Training Facility
Salinas Valley State Prison
Pleasant Valley State Prison
Avenal State Prison

CSP Corcoran
Substance Abuse Treatment Facility and State Prison

California Men's Colony

North Kern State Prison
Wasco State Prison

California Correctional Institution
CSP Los Angeles County

California Institution for Men
California Institution for Women
California Rehabilitation Center

Ironwood State Prison
Chuckawalla Valley State Prison

Calipatria State Prison

Richard J. Donovan Correctional Facility

Centinela State Prison

Sacramento
Vacaville
San Francisco
Stockton
Tracy
Jamestown
Chowchilla
Salinas
Fresno
San Luis Obispo
Bakersfield
Santa Barbara
Los Angeles
Chino
Riverside
Blythe
San Diego
El Centro

120

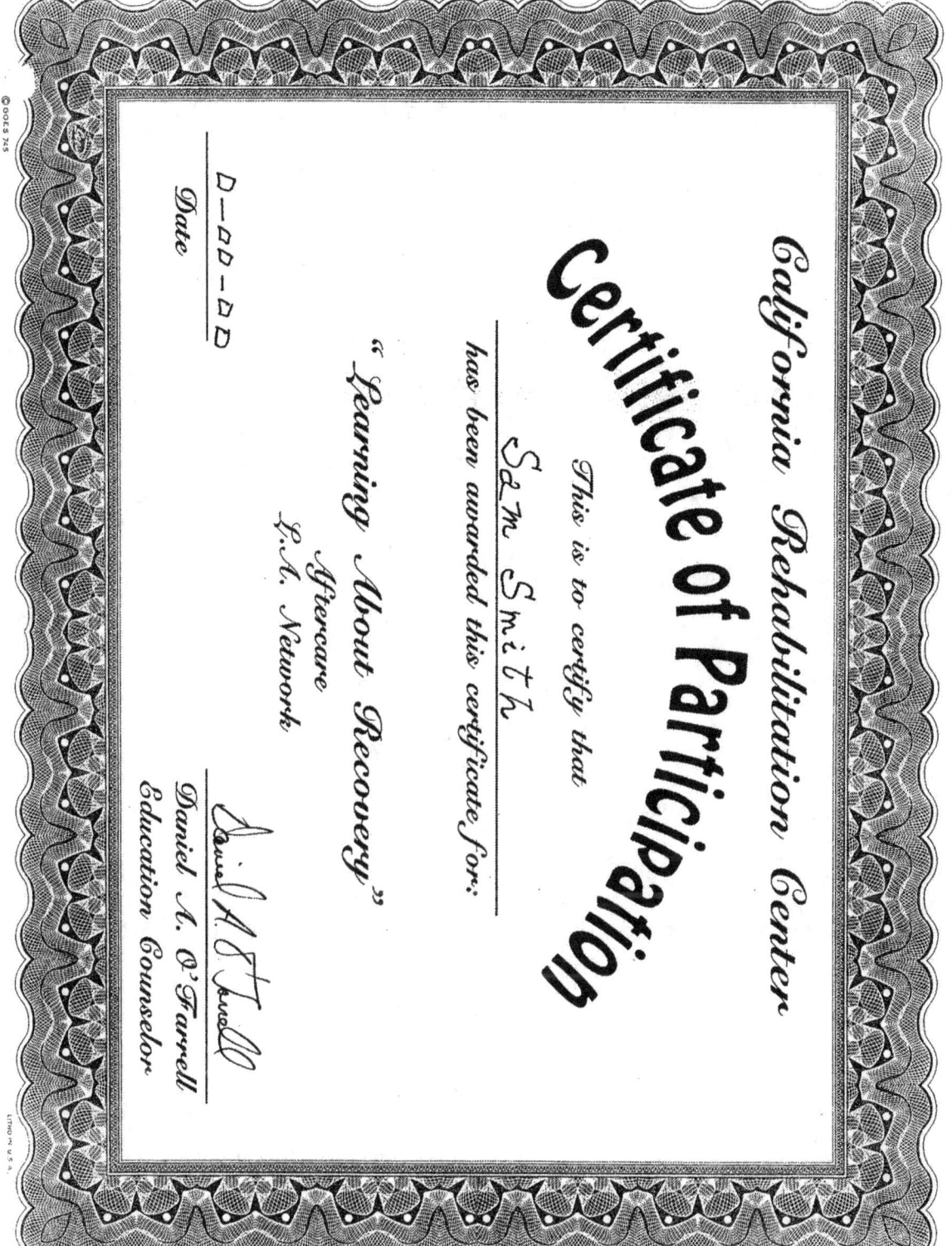

California Rehabilitation Center

Certificate of Participation

This is to certify that

has been awarded this certificate for:

Sam Smith

"Learning About Recovery"

Aftercare
L.A. Network

D-DD-DD
Date

Daniel A. O'Farrell
Education Counselor

121

THE LA PRISON PROJECT NETWORK

The Los Angeles Prison Project Network, also known as LAPPN or LA Network, provides substance abuse treatment and recovery services to selected men and women released from CRC who reside in Los Angeles County.

There are seven service providers within the LAPPN. The Program began at CRC in 1992. It was further strengthened by the Institution when Tarzana TX Center was appointed to administer the LAPPN Program, and also strengthened in 1995 when onsite offices were established on both the Men's and Women's sides of CRC. It is felt this progressive move has enhanced communication and aided the placement of persons into a structured program upon release.

LA Network is primarily about lowering Re*cidivism*. Recidivism, as you all know, is that Five Dollar word that means rearrest, bringing parolees back to CRC as Parole Violators because they have not been able to comply with the rules of Parole in Society. LA Network has enjoyed an average rate of 36% reduction in recidivism of LAPPN Parolees over the past four years.

Our work is scheduled at the latter part of an Inmate's sentence so that the *focus* on Re*lease* will not take away from the *focus* on *Education* in substance abuse, Relapse Prevention and Domestic and other violence. We hope it aids in producing a "Structured Program" that the Parolee takes with Him or Her when they leave CRC. Our work follows your work which is specifically designed to address serious drug addiction and the criminal act or acts it has caused. Our work is programmed for the last 3 to 4 months of the inmates stay at CRC. The inmate makes a six-month commitment to our program as an *In-Patient, Out-patient* or *Sober Living House resident*. All three modalities are usually used during the six months of structured parole.

We have 23 Treatment Centers in Los Angeles County represented by the seven Providers who make up the Network, and come to CRC every other week to do *focused Group*. They are:

1. *Impact House* in Pasadena, CA,

2. *Pacifica House* in Hawthorne, CA,

3. *Cry Help/ Socorro* in Hollywood, CA,

4. *Tarzana Treatment* in the San Fernando Valley (coordinator of the LA Network Program),

5. *Sobriety House* in Long Beach, CA,

6. *Phoenix House* in Venice, CA,

    and

7. *Special Services Group (SSG)* in South Central Los Angeles (This Group represents 15.Tx Centers in the Los Angeles County area).

State and County funds are what make up the LAPPN Budget. The inmate must have earned a *Letter of Acceptance* to the designated Treatment Center by participating in a Biweekly Group here at CRC, and demonstrating manners, other proper behavior, and a general desire to lead a clean and sober life-style back in Society.

Classes at the different Treatment Centers include a full continuum of Care such as:

*Medical Detoxification (they shouldn't need that from here.)

*Residential Rehabilitations Services

*Outpatient Services

*Partial Hospitalization

*Adolescent Services for Family

*Psychiatric Services

*Assessment and Referral

*Specialized Services for Women and Children

*Specialized HIV/AIDS Services

*Drug Education (including Smoking Cessation)

*12-Step Meetings

*Crisis Intervention

*Aftercare (Tarzana has 19 Sober Living Houses)

*Primary Care Medical Services

    and

*Drug Court affiliation

As of February of this year, the LA Network was also given permission by CRC to work with Felon Numbers as well as N-Number Violators. So far, so good!

Transportation from CRC to the Treatment Center upon Parole is coordinated with the Inmate's CCI following Prison Board approval and Bed/Space verification. ALL LAPPN Tx Centers are consistently full, but CRC enjoys assigned bed VIP status.

Just a final thought upon closing and taking questions, Former Chief Justice Warren Burger has written: "The act of go*ing* to prison can, for many inmates, be punishment enough. Once there, they should be allowed to advance their education and learn job skills to help them to be productive citizens back in Society."

We believe that, and appreciate being here at CRC, and a part of the *Team Approach* to overall coaching and training used here. Every day here for every inmate is another step toward a clean and sober, crime-free lifestyle. And it daily proves our profound belief that *"Incarceration without Education is just doing time."* Thank you.

Questions please.

Integrated Behavioral Healthcare

Date:_____

To Whom It May Concern:

This letter will serve to verify that

_____,CDC # _____,
has been conditionally accepted into Tarzana Treatment Center's
Chemical Dependency Program.

An assessment prior to admission will be required to determine the
mode of service recommended.

All services are contingent based upon availability.

If _____, CDC #_____
can not be placed with our program, Tarzana Treatment Center will
refer the client to another Prison Project Network Program affiliate or
community organization.

If we can be of any further assistance, feel free to contact me at
909-273-2924, or contact Pat Hickey, Tarzana Treatment Center, at
818-996-1051 ext. 127

Respectfully,

Dan O'Farrell
Case Manager/Educational Counselor
CIU Program Coordinating Services

AFTER CARE

ATTENTION ALL FELON NUMBERS
GOOD NEWS !

IF YOU WILL BE PAROLING TO REGION III, LOS ANGELES COUNTY, WE CAN HELP YOU FIND A PLACE TO LIVE WHICH WILL HELP YOU TO DISCHARGE SUCCESSFULLY FROM PAROLE. THE L.A. PRISON PROJECT NETWORK OFFERS THE FOLLOWING:

1. IN-PATIENT RESIDENTIAL: BOARD AND ROOM PROVIDED AT NO COST

2. OUT-PATIENT: YOUR PRIVATE ADDRESS

3. SOBER LIVING HOUSE: USUALLY OPERATED BY TREATMENT CENTER. YOU GO BACK TO WORK, PAY RENT, AND ATTEND YOUR AA OR NA MEETINGS.

L.A. PRISON PROJECT NETWORK IS NOW ACCEPTING FELONS AS WELL AS N-NUMBER VIOLATORS.

WE ARE OPEN 5 DAYS PER WEEK, FROM: 9:00AM UNTIL 4:00PM, MONDAY THROUGH FRIDAY.

WE PREFER THAT YOU HAVE AT LEAST TWO TO THREE MONTHS REMAINING HERE, SO THAT YOU ARE ABLE TO ATTEND GROUP MEETINGS CONDUCTED BY L.A. NETWORK HEALTH PROVIDERS FROM LOS ANGELES COUNTY. HOPE TO SEE YOU SOON!

DAN O'FARRELL
EDUCATION COUNSELOR
L.A. PRISON PROJECT NETWORK (LAPPN)
EXT. 2924

THE SALVATION ARMY
HARBOR LIGHT CENTER

809 East 5th Street
Los Angeles Ca. 90013
(213) 626-4786

MEN

HARBOR LIGHT is a 90 day to one year residential program. We provide **FOOD, SHELTER AND TREATMENT** for men seeking freedom from **ALCOHOL AND DRUG** abuse/addiction. **HARBOR LIGHT** treats the whole person.........**BODY, MIND AND SPIRIT!**

Services provided are as follows:

* 24 hour intake	* Male Sexuality	* G E D
* Social Model Detox	* Alcohol/Drug Ed.	* Re-Entry Phase
* Family Sessions	* Relapse Prevention	* Bible Study
* Referrals (as needed)	* Step Study/Big book	* Chapel Services
* CO-dependency	* 12 Step mtgs.	
* Domestic Violence	* Life Skills	
* Sexual Abuse		

* We have Certified Addiction Specialist on staff to provide counseling.
  We also have a Chaplain to provide spiritual guidance.

* No one is <u>TURNED AWAY</u> for lack of funds!!!
                We treat Dual-Diagnose clients!

Attitude

The longer I live, the more I realize the impact of attitude on life. Attitude, to me, is more important than facts. It is more important than the past, than education, than money, than circumstances, than failures, than successes, than what other people think or say or do. It is more important than appearance, giftedness or skill. It will make or break a company... a church... a home. The remarkable thing is we have a choice everyday regarding the attitude we will embrace for that day. We cannot change our past... we cannot change the fact that people will act in a certain way. We cannot change the inevitable. The only thing we can do is play on the one string we have, and that is our attitude... I am convinced that life is 10% what happens to me and 90% how I react to it. And so it is with you... we are in charge of our attitudes.

Written by: Charles S. Windoll

Commitment

Commitment is what transforms a promise into a reality. It is the words that speak boldly of your intentions and the actions that speak louder than words. It is making the time when there is none. It's coming through time after time, year after year after year. Commitment is the stuff character is made of, the power to change the fact of things. It is the daily triumph of integrity over skepticism.

CALIFORNIA DEPARTMENT OF CORRECTIONS

CRC PRE-RELEASE CENTER

INMATE INFORMATION HANDOUT

Sober Living Environment Specialists
A Partnership

The Creation & Management of an R-4

Sober living House

Daniel A. O'Farrell

FOREWORD

On the first morning after my first day managing an R-4 Sober Living House, I was awakened at 6:30 a.m. by two Orange County Marshalls at my bedroom door.

Apparently two, escaped, convicted bank robbers from Atlanta, Georgia had given our House address as their former residence. The entire House was surrounded by Marshalls with loaded rifles aimed at the House.

I introduced myself; said "No, they were not here," and that I had never heard of them before. I told them it was my first day on the job as a House Manager, but that I was a full-time Alcohol and Drug Abuse Counselor.

"Well, I guess you know what you're getting into," one said smiling. "We get tips on fugitives living in these houses all the time. This one looks like a good one though," he said, as they both departed.

Whew!

INTRODUCTION

The disease of alcoholism directly affects the lives of millions of people. It indirectly drains vitality and productivity from the whole of society.

Deteriorating health, the loss of a job, financial chaos and the loss of family and friends usually puts a man on the street. A good, 90-day rehabilitation program at a rehab house or a hospital can put this person on his way back to a productive life. However, a great gap, or drop-off point seems to be looming at the recovering person's commencement ceremony from treatment……..where does he now go with a head full of *AA* and a desire to change? The old neighborhood, the old friends, the same friendly bar? It doesn't usually work. This same person can end up very quickly, as the old saying goes, with the head still full of *AA*, but with the belly full of whiskey; a diametrical collision course!

This is the point where the *R-4 House*, with a small support group of fellow-recovering residents, can be one of the most important steps this person takes. The alcoholic is difficult to reach in the first place, and even in recovery his treatment can create big problems.

Progress is being made toward understanding the complex nature of the disease. Recovering alcoholics can be very rigid, and hard to train. But most alcoholics can be understood, and with understanding help, can break out of the rigid and stereotyped patterns of self-destructive behavior toward a constructive and fruitful life once again.

The alcoholic is difficult to keep in treatment. The results of treatment in many cases have been minimal and discouraging. Only in recent years have the medical, psychological and sociological professions become willing to accept this problem as an illness, and actively search for effective treatment methods. This interest has been sparked by the increasing rate of alcoholism throughout the world, and the ever-increasing burden on country, state and federal institutions attempting to cope with it as a major problem in our society. Specific, researched programs for treating alcoholism and other drug dependencies have, of necessity, been organized and implemented with encouraging results.

The initial primary 28 or 30-day treatment program is designed to sober the alcoholic up, and give him some knowledge of his disease, and tools with which to work on himself. Primary treatment usually follows a three to seven-day detoxification effort, if detox is required. The next stage is usually a 60-day program of additional classwork on the diseases and different dependencies. Suggested techniques and behavior modification patterns designed to help the dependent person are offered to help gain and sustain sobriety.

One of the most difficult problems in treating alcoholism is their unwillingness to surrender to the problem; to admit they are alcoholic and then seek help. The alcoholic _must_ recognize that he can't do it alone, and that he has been incapable of solving his own problems. The surrendering process is not a one-time event, and must be repeated several times. A person will usually hit bottom, develop the proper amount of humility or demoralization, surrender to others, and _then_ seek treatment.

It is after this treatment that an *R-4 Sober Living House* can become a vital, structured aid to the alcoholic's continued struggle to <u>maintain</u> serenity and sobriety. His salvation literally lies in keeping his ego reduced and staying humble. It is incredibly important that the alcoholic not leave treatment too early, and that he avoids a "Superman Urge" sometimes referred to as the "Perfectionist-Failure Bind" in the psychological sense.

Many alcoholics strive for perfection during recovery to make up for past unacceptable behavior. Because of their desire for perfection, they can build in failure for themselves to make mistakes and to be human. To avoid becoming bitter, angry and disillusioned, he must surround himself with meaningful, interpersonal relationships. Thus joining the *Fellowship of Alcoholics Anonymous* (and other self-help groups such as NA, CA, OEA, etc.), becomes therapeutic. By becoming a tenant of an *R-4 Sober Living House*, he might be able to find the structured, positive support he needs to deal with the complexities of life, and continue the fight for sobriety. He is allowed to do this on a daily basic with understanding friends, and with a complete recognition of reality.

OPERATIONS

The R-4 Sober Living House is a business. Tenants must pay rent, usually in advance, to live there. There are structured rules and regulations for living in the House, which are usually agreed to in writing. These rules and regulations usually give the House Manager the right to immediately dismiss a tenant from the House with no reason necessary for rule infractions. The residents can't drink, can't use, can't bring girlfriends into their rooms at night, can't be boisterous or threatening to fellow tenants, and in general must act like human beings. Common sense is the key formula for successful *R-4* living.

Attitudes that range from "don't give a damn" to "control freak" must be modified. One can imagine the degree of anxiety a new tenant just out of treatment will have......... impulsive, short-sighted mannerisms, feelings of fear and frustration, failure and vulnerability are common. A desire to once again escape, or return to the bottle must be recognized and diverted. Poor judgment in dealing with fellow tenants is normal, and must be addressed and corrected. The magic drug that once allowed him to see the world through rose-colored glasses is gone, and Mr. Happy-Go-Lucky Nice Guy can now become belligerent, scared; feel inadequate, not up to the task; and definitely not understood by anyone! His attitude will change if he begins to understand he's in a "safe place," with people like himself, who want and <u>can</u> help him. Much of the help in a *Sober Living House* is freely given by other tenants who have basically become "role models" in dressing properly, bathing properly, going to work, and in general doing what has to be done. By expressing positive, friendly feeling toward the new tenant and others (like we all should do anyway!), by "showing up, suiting up, and being up," supportive fellow tenants can be of tremendous help to one another. It counters isolation and loneliness for all concerned.

<u>ROOM ASSIGNMENT</u>

A typical, four-bedroom house will accommodate eight residents, with house manager usually living in a comfortable, converted garage or "added room" that used to be part of the patio. It's important to be cognizant of any prejudices or built-in animosities or irritabilities a potential resident may have, as will usually be revealed in the intake interview. Some other fellows, for example, might not want to room with younger fellows, and vice-versa. No overcrowding in bedrooms should be allowed. Two residents per normal size bedroom is recommended. Four bunk beds in one average size bedroom will cause more problems than help, and will lead to tenants fighting and leaving.....and the possible closing of the House by the city authorities if legitimate complaints are acted upon. Overcrowding is also the first sign of the "greed factor," where bottom-line profit is the sole purpose of the House. This happens often to entrepreneur-oriented people who started the House with spirituality in mind, and then succumbed to the chance to increase bucks. This type of situation is antithesis to the term "Sober Living."

CHORES

A chore list is attached in the Appendix as Exhibit "A." Each member should be assigned a duty for both his own recovery, and to keep expenses down. The House Manager should be fair in assigning these chores (newest tenant gets the bathroom!), and non-abrasively strict to make sure these chores get done on a timely basis. The quality of chore work can make or break a good House. Good tenants in recovery need, want, and demand a clean House. Hence, a House Manager is extremely derelict in his role as manager and in his understanding of recovery if he does not enforce good House rules and regulations.

MANNERS

Residents in recovery must constantly work on being gentlemen. Rules and regulations spelling some of these character behavior methods out should be posed in the House rule area. (Please see Exhibit "B") These rules must be treated very seriously by the House Manager, and not allowed to be taken lightly. No abrasive language *at* someone, wearing shirts at all times when in the front yard, no terribly loud music, cleaning up after one's self in the kitchen and bathrooms, understanding that borrowing someone else's food without the permission is *stealing*, etc., are all types of manners and behavior modifications that must be constantly worked on and appreciated. A House that tries to follow common sense rules is usually a happy House, and a good place to live. Car maintenance, personal hygiene, clean clothing, a positive attitude, paying your rent on time along with assuming other areas of proper responsibility being a good and *quiet* neighbor and fellow citizen all play a keen role in successful operation of a quality *Sober Living House*.

THE NEIGHBORHOOD

The type of neighborhood in which the House is located is extremely important to the success of the House. The House should be located in a quiet, neighborhood setting, near shopping and medical offices. Many people in recovery don't have cars, so close proximity to bus stops or the Metro-Rail is a good idea. If possible, the Houses should be relatively close to freeways so people can get to work and job interviews. Nearby community parks with tennis courts or basketball courts are a plus. Recovering people need exercise and usually want it. Picnic areas and walking or jogging trails are helpful for meditation and exercise. The picnic areas are a good place to entertain visiting family, or new friends. Recovering people need to get back into neighborhoods and enjoy being good citizens again. A House Manager or owner's worst nightmare is for the neighbors to feel there's a bunch of drunks and drug addicts living down the street! It's unfair to the neighborhood and it certainly won't help the self esteem or economic success of the House and its inhabitants.

RENT

Rent in a good House in Orange County is usually between $70 and $95 per week, paid in advance, and backed by a one-week security deposit. The House Manager *must* keep ahead of the tenant. Many residents leave in the middle of the night with all of their scarce belongings due to other pressures, both social, financial and legal. Residents have consistently been good at leaving when their bill gets over $400 or $500.

Monthly assessments of $5 to $10 per tenant will usually take care of bathroom tissue, paper towels, and kitchen mop and wax materials. Cable TV hookups to each room are the norm now, and usually run an additional $5 per month per tenant. A local newspaper can be delivered to the House for an extra charge of $1 per month per tenant. All utilities and a gardener are included in the rent. A pay phone, mounted in the House, is recommended and precludes disastrous, unpaid bills to Iowa, New York, Peking and elsewhere.

THE HOMELESS

It is important to note that the homeless are now a major problem *and* opportunity in the *Sober Living House* industry in America.

Researchers on homelessness now largely agree that far too little housing stock is now available for homeless people.[9]

Although estimates vary considerably, little disagreement exists that special efforts are needed now and in the immediate future to *create* low income housing to *replace* low-

[9] *A Guide to Housing For Low Income People Recovering From Alcohol And Other Drug Problems* – National Institute on Alcohol Reform and Alcholism, January, 1991, page 14. U.S. Dept. of Human Services and Public Health.

income housing that has been lost. Additional housing is particularly critical for homeless people with alcohol and other drug problems, who are over-represented among the displaced (*Belcher and DiBlasio, re footnote 1, 1990, page 26.*). Alcohol and other drug recovery programs must continue serving low-income people to counteract this displacement, or we will continue to see homeless clients recycling through our programs. Losses of SRO housing, (*Coalition for the Homeless 1985*) and rooming houses, which for decades had accommodated low income, single men with drinking problems, have been particularly severe.[10] Losses of these types of housing over the past 20 years appears to be well over 50% in major metropolitan areas.

A second loss has been the closing of protective institutional settings, usually for chronic drinkers, such as alcoholic wards at state hospitals and county jail farms. Swept away in reform movements to improve mental health services and decriminalize alcoholism and discounted houses as inappropriate housing at the time, institutional settings were swept away along with in-community SRO's and rooming houses.[11]

Institutional facilities have not been replaced. Instead, in the last years of the 1980's, we have seen new appreciation for the fact that these earlier institutions were, for all their shortcomings, usually preferable to the streets, shelters, sobering stations, and the detoxification centers that have come to take their place. Many professionals are now calling for reinstitutionalization, particularly for those with both mental health and alcohol and other drug problems.[12]

The days of the inexpensive SRO and informally-operated boarding houses have passed, as have those of the state hospital and the county jail farm; these facilities are not likely to be rebuilt. *Some form of managed housing still must be supplied for very-low-incoming people with alcohol and other drug problems.*[13]

[10] Same reference as above – page 16.
[11] Same reference as above – page 18.
[12] Same reference as above – page 20.
[13] Same reference as above – page 28.

CONCLUSION

Over the past decade, health services have shifted from the in-patient to the out-patient; from the day-care to the drop-in; from the clinic to the emergency room; and from the detoxification ward to the sobering station. Outreach efforts and referrals for mental health and social services have been sharply reduced. Readily available, inexpensive hotels, clothes, food and day-job agencies have been replaced by one-night shelters, feeding programs, liquor stores, and street-corner hiring. Crime and trauma rates have increased and on-street drug-dealing have skyrocketed in once-tranquil neighborhoods.

The *R-4 Sober Living House, run by the private sector as a business*, can be a great answer and progressive hope to this social evolution brought on by hard financial times, misdirected government programs and priorities, exploding population, *and* a new general awareness, maybe brought about by the mass media (particularly by television) that we *do* have a problem and therefore a responsibility. Ninety days in a rehabilitation center or hospital is great. But we *can't* drop these people off the end of the earth at the end of the 90 days. As stated before, there really is nothing worse or more traumatic and debilitating as a head full of *AA* and a belly full of whiskey. This scenario is a rehabilitation, developmental nightmare! The 90 days is basically useless if the client or resident is returned to the same dysfunctional neighborhood or the street.

Inexpensive, clean rooms inhabited by supportive, clean, resident tenants, all with a common goal of sobriety, can be a passive giant in the final step of true, sustained recovery. Ninety days is not enough. Some rehabilitation experts are now suggesting six-month stays for men and as much as a year for recovering women in orderly, structured, rehab environments.

We all know that high costs alone makes this impossible for hospitals and rehabilitation centers. The demand for shelter and help has never been greater just in sheer numbers.

Imperative in the *R-4 Sober Living House* operation fulfilling this need is their unequivocal necessity to stay honest......that means *clean, sober* and *respectable.* There is no room for the greed factor. Normal, decent profits are readily available. Soul and spirituality must exist in the House as role-modeled by the House Managers and owner/ operators. *No* shooting up in the bathrooms; no drinking in the garages; and no women coming in through the windows at 2:00 a.m.! This is a serious business for serious people. Recovering alcoholics and abusers of other drugs can find serenity and sustained sobriety in a properly run House. House managers with a background in property management and at least some academic training in alcohol and drug abuse programs can provide a great service to the Fellowship by walking the walk, talking the talk, and practicing and displaying *rigorous honesty* in the management of these Houses.

The economic rewards can be very fruitful. Incomes in excess of $100,000 annually are being achieved right now by owner/operators of multiple Houses that are honestly operated and maintained. The *personal* rewards of continuing sobriety and remaining clean and sober, of course, are the intrinsic returns that no one can *buy* or *give* to one's self. These rewards are earned by giving back to our fellow man, regaining our dignity, and once again becoming honest, happy, productive members of our great society.

BIBLIOGRAPHY

1. *Drugs and the Human Body* – Ken Liska, MacMillan Publishing Co., New York, Third Edition, Copyright 1981, 1986 and 1990.

2. *Loosening the Grip* – Kinney and Leatson, Mosbey Year Book, Inc., Fourth Edition, Copyright 1991.

3. *Guide to Housing for Low Income People Recovering From Alcohol and Other Drug Problems. A* – National Institute on Alcohol Reform and Alcoholism, Published in January 1991, U.S. Dept. of Human Services and Public Health.

EXHIBIT "A"

CHORES

		Assigned To:
Kitchen	Counter Floor	- -
Front Room and Halls		- -
Shower Room		- -
Trash and Garbage		- -
Yard and Garage		- -

KITCHEN

1. Absolutely no grease will be poured down the sink drain. Grease can is under kitchen sink.

2. Kitchen counter – Each person is responsible for washing his dishes and putting them back in kitchen cabinet after each meal…..immediately after

147

eating. It's a mess for everybody else otherwise. Absolutely NO EXCUSES will be tolerated on this in the interest of good hygiene.

3. Over stove – Please clean up your own mess on burners after using oven.

4. Bathrooms – Nine to ten people use these bathrooms. Please clean up after yourself and leave it for the next person like you'd like to find it. Thank you.

FRONT ROOM

1. Vacuum rugs and carpet in front room area and hallways

   A. Keep cushions and pillows neat and orderly

   B. Empty and wash ashtrays

   C. Trash newspapers daily or place in recycling box

   D. Spot clean carpet for accidental spills, etc.

   E. Dust furniture – Wax or polish floor and furniture 1st Sat. each month

   F. Wash and dust around kitchen area

SHOWER ROOM

DAILY:

   A. Empty and clean ashtray and wastebasket

   B. Shake out rugs (outside please) on Wed. and Sat.

   C. Keep rooms picked up and clean

148

D.   Clean up any hair left from self-administered barbering

SUNDAY:

A.   Shower room crew GI entire bathrooms

B.   Scour bathtub, sink, shower stall and commode

C.   Clean mirror

D.   Sweep and mop floor. (Clean counters) Get the corners!

DAILY:

A.   Empty trash and garbage cans

B.   Empty lint box by dryer in garage

C.   If it's trash or garbage, and not in a container, get it to the outside garbage cans.

D.   Trash all newspapers older than one day or place in recycle box

E.   Trash pickup – Put garbage cans outside on front street before 7:30 a.m. on Tuesday mornings.

YARD AND GARAGE

1.   Keep front and backyard picked up and neat

A.   Water all shrubbery on Saturday or Sunday

B.   Wear a shirt at all times when working in *front yard*

C.   No parking on the lawn

D.   Minor work only on cars in front yard area. Please overhaul it somewhere else.

2.   Keep the garage looking neat and orderly; some expensive baggage and other personal items are usually stored here. House Manager has the *only* key.

3.   Absolutely *No Unauthorized Items* will be put in garage at any time. This is grounds for dismissal from the House.

EXHIBIT "B"

MANNERS

READ AND HEED!

1. The kitchen, front room and shower room are high density areas. It is everyone's responsibility to leave these areas in better shape than they found them.

2. Everyone keeps the *whole* House clean. Chore people keep it spotless.

3. All chore areas will get a major cleaning on Sat. and Sun.

CABINETS, REFRIGERATORS AND CLOSET

Shelf assignments

1.	
2.	
3.	
4.	
5.	
6.	
7.	
8.	
9.	

Shelf	

Do not borrow food without *expressed permission*. Borrowing without permission is *STEALING*, and you will be asked to leave the House if this occurs. House Manager is *sole* determinator of what happens on this.

If any food or personal items are placed in any but "authorized areas," these items will be disposed of.

NO EXCUSES!

BASIC STARTUP INVENTORY FOR AN R-4 *SOBER LIVING HOUSE*

Lawn furniture – umbrella table	1 ea
Twin beds (Frame, box, mattress)	5 ea
Dressers or chest of drawers	2 ea
Refrigerators	2 ea
Kitchen set	1 ea
Kitchen utensils, pots, pans, plates, etc.	
Toaster	1 ea
Blender	1 ea
Couches	4 ea
End tables	4 ea
Cocktail tables	2 ea
TV l(19" or 20")	2 ea
Clocks	2 ea
Telephones	3 ea
Wastebaskets	7 ea
Vacuum cleaner	1 ea
Pictures (wall)	8 ea
Drapes and rods	6 sets
Lamps	13 ea
Microwave	1 ea
Desk (and 2 desk chairs)	1 ea
Mirrors	5 ea
Rug and pad (approx. 24" by 24"0	1 ea
Nightstands	*6 ea*

Approx. cash outlay $3,000

(Purchase items at garage sales,

thrifts, Salvation Army, etc.

Offer donation tax write-off

to whomever)

in Los Angeles County

TARZANA TREATMENT CENTERS

18646 Oxnard Street, Tarzana, California 91356

CENTRAL INTAKE UNIT

COORDINATING AGENCY

The LAPSN consists of six (6) community based treatment agencies that provide the following services to all eligible parolees with a history of chemical dependency:

1. Residential Substance Abuse Treatment

2. Structured Outpatient Treatment

3. Transition or Sober Living Facilities

4. Transportation upon Release from CRC to a PSN Provider

Services Offered are designed to assist parolees returning to the community to live healthy and productive lives.

You are eligible if you will parole into Los Angeles County from California Rehabilitation Center or Adelanto Correctional Facility and any other California correctional facility or if you are already on parole in Los Angeles County.

TARZANA TREATMENT CENTER'S Central Intake Unit provides outreach, education, assessment and orientation on site at CRC and refers you to an appropriate treatment provider. While you are incarcerated, the treatment provider representative will meet with you on a regular basis.

If you are at CRC, contact your correctional counselor or call us at (909) 273-2924.

If you are on parole, you or your agent call us at (818) 996-1051, ext. 1121 or 3845. Or Call any of the agencies listed on the reverse side. In addition, you may FAX us at (818) 654-3868

Tarzana, CA 91356

(818) 996-1051 ext. 3845 or 1127

Mike d'Agostin or Concepcion Garcia

Substance Abuse Foundation of Long Beach

3125 E. 7th Street

Long Beach, CA 90804

(562)439-7755

Socorro/Cri-Help, Inc.

5110 Huntington Drive

Los Angeles, CA 90032

(323) 343-9530

Richard Block

The Salvation Army, Inc.

809 East 5th Street

Los Angeles, CA 90013

(323) 461-2746

Kevin Kildow

Pacifica House/Behavioral Health Services

2501 W. El Segundo Avenue

Hawthorne, CA 90250

(323) 754-2816

Thomas Bucciarelli

Southern California Alcohol and Drug Programs, Inc.

11500 Paramount Blvd.

Downey, CA 90241

(562) 923-4545, Ext. 239

Oscar Cardena

Phoenix House, Inc.

503 Ocean Front Walk

Venice, CA 90291

(310) 392-3070

Ask for the LAPSN Representative

CDC 1286 (6/97)

WHO IS ELIGIBLE FOR WORKERS' COMPENSATION?

All inmates are eligible for workers' compensation benefits for an injury, illness, or death which occurs while engaged in ASSIGNED WORK. ASSIGNED WORK is defined as designated labor which is performed for the benefit of the California Department of Corrections (CDC). No benefits are due if an inmate is injured as the result of an assault in which the inmate is the initial aggressor. No benefits will be paid if the inmate intentionally injures himself/herself.

NO DISABILITY BENEFITS ACCRUE OR ARE DUE WHILE AN INMATE IS INCARCERATED.

HOW ARE BENEFITS OBTAINED?

The inmate must report IMMEDIATELY to the work supervisor. If the injury requires treatment other than first aid, the inmate will be sent to the institution hospital.

In appropriate, the supervisor will report the injury to the State Compensation Insurance Fund (SCIF0), a CDC adjusting agent.

Upon release from prison, SCIF is responsible for overseeing provision of benefits.

Any delay in reporting the injury may prevent an inmate from receiving benefits.

WHAT BENEFITS ARE AVAILABLE?

Benefits may include medical treatment, disability payments, vocational rehabilitation or death benefits.

WHO ADMINISTERS MEDICAL CARE?

CDC has control over medical treatment provided to an incarcerated inmate. In the case of a serious injury, the inmate can request a consulting physician who is selected by the Department.

Upon release from prison, the inmate may chose his/her own physician.

WHEN ARE DISABILITY PAYMENTS MADE?

1. Medical temporary disability exists after the release, and/or

2. The inmate sustained permanent disability due to the ASSIGNED WORK injury, and/or

3. The inmate is unable to perform the work he/she was doing when injured and participants in vocational rehabilitation.

WHAT IS THE PROCEDURE IF A DISPUTE EXISTS?

Where there is a dispute regarding the inmate's right to workers' compensation benefits, the inmate may file an application with the Workers' Compensation Board or they may consult an attorney of their choice.

Additional information about the workers' compensation process and benefits may be obtained by contacting the Office of Benefits Assistance and Enforcement. This information will be provided at no charge by the State Division of Workers' Compensation. Their address as well as the address of the SCIF office may be found in local city directories.

_____

_____

	Number:
Department of Corrections	91/2
INFORMATIONAL BULLETIN	Date Issued: December 19, 1990
Subject: PAROLEE BENEFITS INFORMATION	Cancelled Effective: February 19, 1991

The purpose of this Informational Bulletin is to take note of and clarify misinformation being obtained by inmates in institutions. Some newly released parolees have unsigned copies of "Benefits from the State of California," and many others have indicated to their parole agents, or through letters to Central Office an awareness of the document and a belief that the listed benefits are available. A sample of the letters and information from the Parole and Community Services Division (P&CSD) indicates a department-wide problem.

Some parolees do qualify for general assistance, food stamps, Supplemental Security Income (SSI) and other benefits. Parolees must meet the same eligibility criteria as applicants not on parole. Examples of benefits which inmates are mistakenly being advised are available through the P&CSD are a $250 clothing allowance, reduced interest Government loans up to $15,000, $2,000 cash for the asking, the entitlement to food, clothing, shelter, medical/dental treatment, employment and transportation while under parole supervision. This has resulted in unrealistic expectations by many parolees and has hindered the development of a positive relationship with parole staff whom they believe are unfairly denying their benefits.

Attached are guidelines and eligibility requirements for basic services available from agencies that may be able to assist ex-offenders. Individual qualifications for program assistance is based on his/her unique circumstances. This information should be disseminated to all parole agents, counselors and pre-release teachers.

Due to the informational nature of this bulletin, it is cancelled 60 days from date of issue. Please inform all persons concerned of the contents of this bulletin. Direct any inquiries regarding this bulletin to Don Foley, Parole Agent III, Parole Headquarters, at (916) 327-1136 or ATSS 467-1136 or Roger Wood, Correctional Counselor II, Education and Inmate Program Unit, Institutions Division, at (916) 445-8035 or ATSS 485-8035.

R.H. Denninger

Chief Deputy Director

Attachment

Informational Bulletin 91/2

Parolee Benefits Information

AGENCY SERVICES/PROCEDURES/ELIGIBILITY REQUIREMENTS

November 1, 1990

SOCIAL SECURITY ADMINISTRATION

The Social Security Administration has two programs – Social Security and Supplementary Security Income (SSI). Social Security does not pay benefits to prisoners while they are incarcerated due to a felony committed after October 1980. SSI does not make payment to inmates in prison or any other prison institution. Aside from these very basic rules which apply to inmates, the programs have very specific eligibility requirements as shown below:

SOCIAL SECURITY

This program does not have any special provisions for ex-felons. This income is financed through Social Security taxes (FICA) providing four main types of insurance benefits. Individuals can qualify for Social Security in one of the following four ways:

○   As a retiree (age 62 or older)

○   As a disabled individual

○   As a survivor of an eligible individual

○   As a dependent of an eligible individual

To qualify for retirement benefits, an individual must have credit for a certain amount of work under Social Security. People can earn a maximum of four credits per year. In 1988, a credit is earned for every $470 of earnings. The number of credits required for retirement is based on the year an individual reaches the age of 62. A person age 62 in 1988 needs 37 credits to retire.

To qualify for disability benefits, an individual must also have credit for a certain amount of work (i.e., credits). In addition, the person must have worked recently under Social Security. The number of credits required depends on your age when you become disabled.

In addition to the work requirements for disability benefits, a person must also be unable to work because of a disability. Social Security considers a person disabled when he or she has a severe physical or mental impairment or combination of impairments that prevents him or her from working for a year or more that is expected to result in death. This definition requires total disability and requires that a person be unable to do any type of work for which they are qualified. NOTE: Being unemployed or incarcerated is not considered a disability.

Survivors benefits can be paid on the account of a deceased worker to:

1.   Unmarried children under the age of 18 or 19 if in high school full-time

2.   An unmarried child disabled before the age of 22

3.   A widow or widower who is caring for a child under the age of 16 or a disabled child

4.   A widow or widower age 60 or older. Benefits may also be paid to widows or widowers 50 or older who are disabled with a disability that started within seven tears of the death of the deceased worker.

5.   Surviving divorced widow or widower.

If an individual is receiving retirement or disability benefits, payments can be made to the following dependents:

1.   Unmarried children under the age of 18 or 19 if in high school full-time

2.   An unmarried child disabled before the age of 22

3.   A wife or husband over the age of 62

4.   A husband or wife who is caring for a child under the age of 16 or a disabled child

5.   A divorced spouse who has been divorced at least two years and who is over the age of 72

Social Security benefits are paid monthly.

SUPPLEMENTAL SECURITY INCOME (SSI)

Again, this program does not have any special provisions for ex-felons. SSI is a program of assistance based on need. Payments can only be made to financially needy persons who are 65 or older, blind, or totally disabled by a medically provable impairment (identical to Social Security disability).

You May Be Owed
Unclaimed Money
To find Out, Enter Your Last Name Here:
SEARCH

A person must be a U.S. citizen or legally admitted alien to qualify for SSI. It is not necessary to have worked to qualify for SSI.

No one can receive SSI while they are in prison or a back payment for periods they were in prison. Prisoners can file for SSI 90 days in advance of their expected release date if they are in an institution with a medical facility.

Parole in America's criminal system

One of today's most hotly debated topics in the criminal justice field is whether or not individual states should abandon the parole system. Many people feel it is time to do away with parole, while others are fighting for its survival. As with any controversial change, there are pros and cons to both sides of the argument, all of which are very convincing. The basic arguments for and against the abolition of the parole system at the state level can be easily defined.

One of the strongest arguments against the destruction of the parole system is the overpopulation problem in most prisons. Since the early 1980's, the population of inmates in correctional institutions has grown astronomically. Between 1986 and 1991, prisons have seen a 41% increase in the population of violent crime offenders. For drug related offenses, the number has increased three-fold. So it would make sense to argue that eliminating parole would make this problem even worse, right? Well, not exactly. Inmate populations are so extreme, that prisoners are sitting on waiting lists. When an inmate is released from prison, the vacant spot is filled instantaneously. In this respect, the parole system is actually doing nothing to fix the overpopulation problem, and increasing operating costs. This was illustrated when between 1976 and 1984, 10 states passed new laws that included the abolition of parole. Only one state, Indiana, had an increase in inmate population. In fact, Minnesota and Washington State both had major reductions in their prisoner populations. The remaining 7 states showed no changes in their inmate population.

The next step in evaluating parole might be to inquire into how the system affects the inmates. Just what effect does parole have on the success of released inmates? Unfortunately, most studies show that it is negative impact. A Bureau of Prisoners (BOP) follow-up investigation of parolees by Miles D.

Harer, Ph.D. displayed some very beleaguering statistics. Of the 1,205 person parolee test group Harer followed in the first half of 1987, over 40% of the former inmates had been rearrested or had their parole revoked. In another study performed in 1989, the National Institute of Justice found that 62% of 180,580 individuals released from prison in 11 different states during 1983 had been rearrested for a felony or serious misdemeanor within a 3-year period. 47% were convicted of a new crime, and 41% were re-incarcerated. A staggering 55% of these parolees were out of work for more than half the year. What is particularly disturbing is that legislation passed in recent years has not helped much. The Tennessee Sentencing Commission (TSI) and the Statistical Analysis Center of the Tennessee Bureau of Investigation performed a study of their parolee population in 1994. The target group consisted of 3,793 people. Of those released during the sample period, around 53% were re-arrested in a 2-year period, with a 39% reincarceration rate.

Another defense of the parole has to do with determining the "bad apples" and focusing special attention on them. Let's identify these "bad apples"; 62% of violent offenders recidivate after release according to a 1989 poll by The Bureau of Justice Statistics. As of December 1998, The Bureau of Prisons ranks drug offenses as the most common transgression with 110,793 prisoners under its jurisdiction. Of these 58,224, 58.6% were drug related. Drug abusers make up the majority of inmates, and the majority of whose parole is rescinded. In one study, the urine of 237 parolee subjects was monitored for SSI payments made monthly. SSI checks are not prepared (or printed) at the Social Security office. Checks are mailed to eligible individuals at their mailing addresses.

DECISION CAN BE APPEALED

You have a right to appeal a decision made on your claim. The first of four appeal steps is a *reconsideration* which gives you an opportunity to submit any evidence not previously considered. You generally have 60 days after receiving a notice you disagree with to file an appeal. For more information about appeal rights, ask at any Social Security office for the leaflet, *Your Right to Question the Decision Made on Your Social Security Claim.*

IF YOUR CLAIM IS APPROVED

Each person whose disability claim is approved will receive a Certificate of Award and a booklet, *Your Social Security Rights and Responsibilities – Disability Benefits.*

MEDICARE

Not to be confused with Medi-Cal or Medicade, Medicare can be applied for through the Social Security Administration. The two parts of Medicare are hospital insurance and medical insurance. They help people 65 and over, disabled persons under 65 who are entitled to Social Security benefits for 24 or more months, and insured workers and their dependents who need dialysis treatment or a kidney transplant because of permanent kidney failure.

The hospital insurance part of Medicare helps pay the cost of inpatient hospital care and certain kinds of follow-up care. The medical insurance part helps pay the cost of doctors services, outpatient services, and for certain other medical items and services not covered by hospital insurance.

People who have medical insurance pay a monthly premium. More than two-thirds of the cost of the medical insurance premium is paid for from general revenues of the Federal government. The basic premium is $33.95 a month through 1989.

If you are eligible for Social Security either as a worker, dependent, or survivor, you are eligible for hospital insurance protection when you are 65. Government employees and certain family members may become eligible for hospital insurance based on the workers' Federal employment.

It is advisable to apply for Medicare three months before your 65th birthday month even if you do not plan to retire. That way your protection will start the month you reach age 65. When you apply for hospital insurance, you will be enrolled automatically for the medical insurance part of Medicare unless you tell them you do not want it.

Persons age 65 and over who have not worked long enough to be eligible for hospital insurance can get this protection by enrolling and paying a monthly premium. The basic premium is $156 a month through 1989. People who buy Medicare hospital insurance must also enroll in medical insurance.

MEDI-CAL

Medi-Cal is California's program to pay for medical care for both public assistance recipients and other low-income persons.

MEDI-CAL (With a Cash Grant)

If you are getting SSI, AFDC (except for some unemployed adults), refugee aid, or In-Home Supportive Services, you are automatically eligible for Medi-Cal. This is sometimes the main reason for applying for these programs even though your income is high enough so that the cash benefits will be small.

There have been many cuts in the Medi-Cal program. For instance, General Assistance/Relief recipients are not eligible for Medi-Cal. Neither are adults between the ages of 18 and 65 who have no dependent children, unless they are disabled. Each person can go to a county health clinic or hospital for medical care.

MEDI-CAL (Without a Cash Grant)

If you are not getting cash welfare, but have low-income and assets worth less than a certain limit, you may also be eligible for Medi-Cal. If you are 65 and over, under 21, disabled or blind, taking care of a child and the other parent is either absent, disabled or unemployed, or if you are pregnant, a refugee or residing in a nursing home, you may be eligible for Medi-Cal under the category Medically Needy.

You must pay the cost of any medical care which is figured to be "your share." Medi-Cal will then pay the rest. If your income is low, your share may turn out to be nothing.

Your car, home and up to $1,500 face value of life insurance are not counted as resources. If you own other real estate with a net market value (market value less what you owe) under $6,000, you do not count it as a current resource, but must sell or rent it within six months.

How to Use Medi-Cal

The State mails eligible persons a Medi-Cal card each month. Always tell the doctor or other health service office that you are using or planning to use Medi-Cal for payment. Some health-care professionals will not accept the card. Authorization from the State is required before many medical services can be performed.

Medi-Cal coverage is always effective from the first of the month in which you apply. If you were eligible for Medi-Cal at any time during the previous three months before applying, you may receive retroactive coverage (for medical service already received).

Medi-Cal will pay bills from outside of California only when an emergency arises due to accidents or illness. Temporary cards are issued by the county welfare offices if you do not get your card, you lose it, or you need more labels in a month.

AFDC recipients who become employed and give up AFDC eligibility may carry medical coverage for four months more.

How to Apply

Go to the county welfare office. Look for the window or office for applying for Medi-Cal. If you are in a hospital, ask the social worker or administrator to help you apply.

What if you have both Medicare and Medi-Cal?

If you have both Medicare and Medi-Cal, Medi-Cal pays Medicare deductibles, premiums and copayments. Medi-Cal also covers many services not covered by Medicare. Therefore, if you are eligible for Medi-Cal, you need not buy supplemental insurance, as it will not provide additional coverage.

County Ability to Pay Services

Counties are required to provide emergency health care. They are required also to provide medical services to low-income people who don't have Medi-Cal. The State pays counties to aid the low-income adults who have been removed in recent years from Medi-Cal by the State government; such as, adults who are not over 65, disabled or have dependent children, but who otherwise meet Medi-Cal's income and resource limits.

Counties may not turn you away because you do not have a copayment. Any charges made by counties must be based on the patient's ability to pay. Counties are not required to provide any minimal range of services. The range of services available varies greatly from county to county.

You will have to fill out some forms, and if your income is very low, you will only have to pay for part of your costs or nothing at all. You must be persistent in requesting the "ability to pay plan." If you have a serious emergency, are about to give birth, or have a contagious disease, you can be seen without paying and can fill out the forms later.

FOOD STAMPS

To qualify for food stamps, you need *not* live in a place where you can cook meals. Food stamps can be used like money at grocery stores to buy food. You can apply for food stamps at your local Welfare Office. Low income is the key. If you are unemployed, work part-time or are on welfare, you qualify. You may also be added to an existing food stamp household. Current maximum for a single individual is $99.90 per month.

Go to your welfare Office with papers and show:

1. Where you are living ("on the street" qualifies)

2. How many in your household

3. How much money you receive each month (gate money is considered)

4. How much you are paying for doctors and rent, if applicable

5. Social Security care or *proof* that you have applied.

It takes approximately 30 days to receive stamps. If you qualify for immediate need, emergency food stamps can be issued within three days.

GENERAL ASSISTANCE

General Assistance (GA) is a county program and the regulations and amounts vary from county to county and is for persons who have no other means of financial support.

You may also apply for food stamps at the same time you apply for GA. If you are eligible for GA, you are eligible for food stamps.

AID TO FAMILIES WITH DEPENDENT CHILDREN (AFDC)

Available to individuals who have children. The family unit may be a one-parent household or, under certain circumstances, a two-parent family. Many counties require certain requirements of the AFDC families to participate in the Greater Avenues for Independence (GAIN) Program. GAIN is designed to get people off welfare through training and education. Child care is provided during the training and education phase.

EMPLOYMENT AND JOB TRAINING

If you are not employed directly, the first week that you are released, you should be sure to become Job Training Partnership Act (JTPA) certified and secure a tax credit voucher. This will increase your employment opportunities. CETA was replaced on September 30, 1983 by the Job Training and Partnership Act. Locate the nearest JTPA office by dialing 1-800-FOR-A-JOB anywhere in California.

As soon as you become JTPA certified, you become qualified to interview for hundreds for JTPA jobs available in your community.

JTPA training varies depending on the occupation and your skill level. At the end of that time, you will have valuable job experience and a reasonable expectation of a permanent job. JTPA positions at companies have normal entry level salaries.

FEDERAL BONDING PROGRAM

EDD offices throughout California are prepared to help job seekers and employers secure fidelity bonding for employees who might be denied coverage by regular commercial carriers. Coverage is available at no cost to the employer or the individual.

CALIFORNIA DEPARTMENT OF REHABILITATION (DOR)

MERELY BEING AN EX-FELON HAS NO CONNECTION WITH QUALIFYING FOR SERVICES

1.   Ex-felons have no special priority with DOR. The qualifications are as follows:

a.   One must have a *physical, mental or learning disability*, but that is *not enough*.

b.   The disability must prevent the client from returning to any jobs he/she has worked at in the past, regardless of whether he/she liked the job or if it "paid enough." In come cases, if that particular job no longer exists in the general job market, and the client has no other marketable skills, he/she *may* quality for retraining. If the client's offense was caused by mental derangement, precluding him/her from returning to work with a specified segment of the population, it *might be* considered as a vocational handicap.

c.   The third criterion is that in view of DOR, if services are provided, the client will be able to gain or maintain employment. This is based on work history and employability, skills, aptitudes and personality.

2.   You do not automatically qualify for rehabilitation services if you are receiving *SSDI* or *SSI*. You must still meet the above criteria (a, b, and c).

3. **GENERAL INFORMATION**

a.	Generally, DOR utilizes public schools for training unless special circumstances exist. Truck driving, for example, is not a good vocational goal for an ex-felon due to employer resistance and insurance considerations, as trainees rarely get hired without hours of on-the-job experience.
b.	DOR does not supply a client with tools if he/she has a trade already. If you meet the above criteria for services and DOR has spoken with the employer who is going to hire you, DOR *may* supply an entry set of tools, if required by the employer.
c.	DOR has nothing to do with loans for clients. DOR does not make loan guarantees or co-sign for loans. If a person is a client with an established vocational goal, DOR *may* authorize direct payment to a department store for clothing for job interviews or work clothes.
d.	Clients use public transportation if they do not possess their own vehicles. DOR *may* cover mileage (usually at 10 cents per mile) for a gasoline allowance to and from training sites. Vehicle purchases are for those people who have no alternative form of transportation, such as a paraplegic or quadriplegic.
e.	DOR provides no grants.
f.	DOR will send someone for specialist examinations, if deemed necessary to establish a disability to qualify them for services with this department.
g.	DOR no longer deals with the Small Business Administration loans. These are between you and the SBA. There are no loan funds available from your DOR counselor. Service Core of Retired Executives (SCORE), however, is an excellent organization to advise someone wanting their own business.

4.   If a parolee meets the eligibility criteria as listed in #1 (a, b and c), they should

contact the DOR Counselor of the Day for telephone screening.

PAROLEE CASH ASSISTANCE

Cash assistance funds are loans to parolees intended to be used when other funds are

not available. The loans are generally for small amounts, under $50, to provide emergency

food, clothing, or shelter while long-term assistance or employment is being arranged.

Cash assistance loans will be submitted to the Parole Agent of Record for review and

approval. The determination of how much money is needed is a matter of judgment, based

on the individual's case circumstances.

KANSAS STATE OPENING PRAYER

April 17, 2001

When Minister Joe Wright was asked to open the new session of the Kansas Senate, everyone was expecting the usual generalities, but this is what they heard.

Heavenly Father, we come before You today to ask Your forgiveness and to seek Your direction and guidance. We know Your Word says, 'Woe to those who call evil good,' but that is exactly what we have done. We have lost our spiritual equilibrium and reversed our values. We confess that we have ridiculed the absolute truth of Your Word and called it Pluralism. We have worshiped other gods and called it multiculturalism. We have endorsed perversion and called it alternative lifestyle. We have exploited the poor and called it the lottery. We have rewarded laziness and called it welfare. We have killed our unborn and called it choice. We have shot abortionists and called it justifiable. We have neglected to discipline our children and called it building self-esteem. We have abused power and called it politics. We have coveted our neighbors' possessions and called it ambition. We have polluted the air with profanity and pornography and called it freedom of expression. We have ridiculed the time-honored values of our forefathers and called in enlightenment. Search us, oh God, and know our hearts today; cleanse us from every sin and set us free. Guide and bless these men and women who have been

set to direct us to the center of Your will and to openly ask these things in the Name of Your Son, The Living Savior, Jesus Christ. Amen.

The response was immediate. A number of legislators walked out during the prayer in protest. In six short weeks Central Christian Church where Minister Wright pastors, logged more than 5,000 phone calls with only 47 of those calls responding negatively. The church is now receiving international requests for copies of this prayer from India, Africa, and Korea. Commentator Paul Harvey aired this prayer on his radio program, "The Rest of the Story," and received a larger response to this program than any other he has ever aired.

With the Lord's help, may this prayer sweep over our nation and wholeheartedly become our desire so that we again can be called "one nation under God."

If you don't stand for something, you'll fall for everything!

Prison Spending in State Budget Draws Criticism

Thursday, Feb. 6, 2003

While schools, healthcare for the poor, and countless other programs are facing drastic cuts in California's state budget, the Department of Corrections is slated to receive a boost. $160 million for a new department headquarters and $220 million to create a state-of-the-art death row center at San Quentin are just two of the line items that have drawn widespread criticism.

On January 22, a state Senate subcommittee met to start cutting back the $5.2 billion prison budget, but many analysts believe that the answer lies in releasing nonviolent offenders and readdressing California's sentencing guidelines.

Only ten years ago, California's prison budget was half of what it is today. Then, there were 109,000 inmates serving time in 24 prisons compared with 160,000 felons incarcerated in 22 prisons today. According to the National Association of Budget Officers, an estimated 7% of state general funds is spent on penal systems, a line item that also covers schools, parks, and healthcare. California, by contrast, spends 9% of its general funds on penal systems.

While "tough on crime" is a popular platform to get voted on regardless of political party affiliation, many elected officials in other states are looking to release prisoners early, revise the parole system, or close prisons rather than have education and healthcare suffer more than necessary as states face severe budget crises.

The problem we face in California, though, is that the California Correctional Peace Officers' Union supported Governor Gray Davis' campaign and is one of our state's most powerful unions. In fact, the Union was the largest campaign donor, contributing $3.4 million to Davis directly and around $1 million in indirect funds. The reality remains that a 26,000-member prison guards union, whose agenda includes tougher sentencing, will directly impact our state's ability to fund education and healthcare adequately.

FAMILY VISITING

Conjugal and family visiting is permitted between individuals and their spouses and members of their immediate family. This process involves careful screening, and visitation must be with approved visitors or with couples who are both housed at the facility.

SELF-HELP GROUPS

There are a number of self-help groups at the facility which the individual may take advantage of on a voluntary basis. These groups are designed to provide a sense of worth and unity among their members as well as assist the members in preparing for release from the institution. Groups meet on a regular basis and each group has a staff sponsor. Active groups currently include Alcoholics Anonymous, Narcotics Anonymous, and Espejo. The community has been very supportive of these groups not only in the institution but also when the individual is released from the institution.

PRE-RELEASE PROGRAM

The facility has a pre-release program to help the individual prepare for release. Many volunteers from the community are involved in the program. Classes are held with the various organizations to try to make the transition from the institution to the community as smooth as possible. Listings of job opportunities throughout the state are available to everyone. Resources in the pre-release program can help individuals secure a driver's license, a job, or housing when they are released.

LEISURE-TIME ACTIVITIES

Many constructive evening and leisure-time activities are provided to assist the individual in learning more effective ways to channel his/her energies. Such activities include basketball, softball, football, handball, weight-lifting, track, aerobics, and other assorted recreational activities. Professional staff direction and guidance are provided.

ADDITIONAL PROGRAMS

The establishment of the federally funded Education Consolidated Improvement Act, Title I programs, adds a new dimension to the academic program. Students under 21 years of age who have been identified by their teachers as needing special help are placed in a specially equipped classroom where they receive individual attention.

One-year period: 119 of the subjects had failed their urine tests, and 27% had already been reincarcerated, only after the first year. A study by Vaillant started in 1973 followed similar subjects for a 20-year period and found 91% of those released went back to drug use in less than 1 year. In 1981, a study performed by Desmond found drug use in 66% of parolees after only 1 week of freedom, and 94% after 1 year. These offenders play a huge role in the burdening of the prison system. Drug offenders accounted for a 44% increase in prison population between 1986 and 1991.

Judging by these statistics, drug abusers, both violent and non-violent, are most at risk to relapse. The reason for this is quite simple. Most of these inmates released on parole never complete any form of rehabilitation program. Proponents of the parole system argue that rehabilitation programs and their success rates make parole a realistic solution. Indeed, there are many great programs that have been started in recent years. For example, the BOP's drug abuse treatment program (DAP), which was started in 1986, has met with astounding results. Parolees who successfully completed this program faced a mere 3.3% chance of being rearrested in the first 6 months after release, and a much lower 20% relapse into drug use. These people faced a 73% lower chance of being rearrested compared to those who did not complete this program. In theory this sounds like the solution to everyone's problems. However, what the many people seem to overlook is the fact that very few parolees actually graduate from any such program. At the time of this 6 month follow-up study, only 1,524 successfully completed the DAP program. The remaining 56,700 imprisoned due to drug related crimes received no such treatment. Studies of all general drug treatment in prisons find only 10% of inmates who need these services actually get them.

The other big question is, just how many taxpayer dollars are used to keep each inmate in prison? Isn't parole more economically sound? It costs from $12,000 a year for federal inmates to remain in prison, to as much as $58,000 a year in New York City. But, how much does it cost the public to deal with parolees who commit new crimes after release? There haven't really been definitive studies performed that compare this cost to that of the monetary value of damage caused by the criminals. This is mainly because of the difficulty to put a price tag on things such as pain and suffering of victims. However, it is widely suspected that the incarceration costs are actually a bargain compared to the costs dealing with the crimes. When it comes to drug related crimes, the cost savings of keeping a criminal incarcerated are quite obvious. A study performed by RAND concluded that substance abuse treatment is up to seven times more cost-effective in reducing some types of drug use than the use of domestic law enforcement. This has also been proven in actual real-world situations. In 1997, The California Department of Corrections (CDC) implemented a new drug treatment program. They have found that for a 200 bed facility such as the Corcroan II saves the CDC 7.5 nearly million dollars over 7 years by reducing abusers' returns to custody. By increasing the program to 3,000 beds, the program would save the state nearly 30 million dollars over the 7 year period. The amount saved is much more than the cost of the program itself.

There is hope that in the future, parole may once more become a viable option when the treatment programs become widely available. Rehabilitation and treatment programs that are preparing inmates for re-entry into society are very successful. However, while such treatment is only dispersed to 10% of those who need it, it's not in the best interest to society to allow these criminals to be released early. More than 2 out of 3 will go right back to a life of crime. Keeping these inmates in prison for the full length of their terms does not increase costs when compared to the costs of releasing them on an unsuspecting public. Also, the prison populations are not adversely effected. Until the remaining 90% of those who need treatment can receive it, it is better for both the public and the inmate for the sentence to be completed as was intended.

Dept. of Health and Public Service

Washington, D.C.

HARMONY HOUSE

HARMONY HOUSE is a model, sober-living, residence for *MEN*, based on the Principles of Alcoholics Anonymous.

We are conveniently located in a quiet residential area, close to bus transportation, movies, restaurants and shopping areas.

We offer:

1.   A supportive environment in a comfortable home like atmosphere.

2.   Pleasant comfortable grounds.

3.   Two men to a room. (No overcrowding).

4.   Kitchen privileges.......Gourmets welcome!!!

5.   Laundry privileges.

6.   Cable TV.

7.   Clean, spacious furnished rooms.

8.   Comfortable living at an affordable price.

<u>We are near to:</u>

A. Huntington Center Shopping Mall.

B. 405 & 22 Freeways.

C. Pacific Ocean Beaches.

D. Mile Square Park with:

- Baseball Diamonds
- Jogging Trails
- Pool & Billiard Tables

- Basketball Courts
- Man Made Lake
- Tennis Courts

- Golf Course
- Picnic Areas
- Night Golf

YOUR CONTRIBUTION

THE WILL TO STAY SOBER

Contact:

Relapse Prevention

Robert R. Perkinson, Ph.D.

There is some bad news about relapse and some good news. The bad news is many patients have problems with relapse in early sobriety. About two thirds of patients coming out of addiction programs relapse within 3 months of leaving treatment (Hunt et al., 1971). The good news is most people that go through treatment ultimately achieve a stable recovery

(Frances, Bucky, & Alexopolos, 1984). Relapse doesn't have to happen to you, and even if it does, you can do something about it. Relapse prevention is a daily program that can prevent relapse. It can also stop a slip from becoming a disaster. This relapse prevention exercise has been developed using a combination of the models of Gorski and Miller (1986) and Marlatt and Gordon (1985). This exercise uses both the disease concept model in combination with a behavioral approach.

RELAPSE IS A PROCESS

Relapse is a process that begins long before you use drugs or alcohol. Certain symptoms precede the first use of chemicals. This relapse prevention exercise teaches how to identify and control these symptoms before they lead to actual drug or alcohol use. If you allow these symptoms to go on without acting on them, serious problems will result.

THE RELAPSE WARNING SIGNS

All relapse begins with warning signs that will signal for you that you are in trouble. If you do not recognize these signs, you will decompensate and finally use chemicals. All of the signs are a reaction to stress, and they are a reemergence of the disease. They are a means by which your body and mind are telling you that you are in trouble. Gorski and Miller (1982) recognized 37 warning signs in patients who had relapsed. You may not have all of these symptoms, but you will have some of them long before you actually use chemicals. You must determine which symptoms are the most characteristic of you, and you must come up with coping skills for dealing with each symptom.

Listed below are the 37 warning symptoms. Circle the ones that you have experienced before you used drugs or alcohol.

1. Apprehension about well-being

2. Denial

3. Adamant commitment to sobriety

4. Compulsive attempts to impose sobriety on others

5. Defensiveness

6. Compulsive behavior

7. Impulsive behavior

8. Loneliness

9. Tunnel vision

10. Minor depression

11. Loss of constructive planning

12. Plans begin to fail

13. Idle daydreaming and wishful thinking

14. Feeling nothing can be solved

15. Immature wish to be happy

16. Periods of confusion

_____

A sponsor or a fellow AA/NA member can warn you when they feel you may be in trouble. Listen to these people. If they tell you they sense a problem, take action. You may need professional help in working the problem through. Don't hesitate in calling and asking for help. Anything is better than relapsing. If you overreact to a warning sign, you are not going to be in trouble, but if you underreact you may be headed for real problems. Chemical dependency is a deadly disease. Your life is at stake.

THE HIGH-RISK SITUATIONS

Marlatt and Gordon (1985) found that relapse is more likely to occur in certain situations. These situations can trigger relapse. They found that people relapsed when faced with life situations that they couldn't cope with except by using chemicals. Your job in treatment is to develop coping skills for dealing with each high-risk situation.

Negative Emotions

Thirty-five percent of people who relapse, relapse when feeling a negative feeling that they can't cope with. Most felt angry or frustrated, but some felt anxious, bored, lonely, or depressed. Almost any negative feeling can lead to relapse if you don't learn how to cope with the feeling. Feelings motivate you to take action. You must act to solve any problem

Circle any of the following feelings that seem to lead you to use chemicals.

1.	Lonely	11.	Envious	21.	Selfish	31.	Scared	41.	Irritated
2.	Angry	12.	Exhausted	22.	Reckless	32.	Spiteful	42.	Overwhelmed
3.	Rejected	13.	Bored	23.	Weak	33.	Sorrowful	43.	Panicked
4.	Empty	14.	Anxious	24.	Sorrowful	34.	Helpless	44.	Trapped
5.	Annoyed	15.	Ashamed	25.	Greedy	35.	Neglected	45.	Unsure
6.	Sad	16.	Bitter	26.	Aggravated	36.	Grieving	46.	Intimidated
7.	Exasperated	17.	Burdened	27.	Enervated	37.	Confused	47.	Distraught
8.	Betrayed	18.	Foolish	28.	Miserable	38.	Crushed	48.	Uneasy
9.	Cheated	19.	Jealous	29.	Unloved	39.	Discontented	49.	Guilty
10.	Frustrated	20.	Left out	30.	Worried	40.	Restless	50.	Threatened

These are just a few of the feeling words; add more if you need to. Develop coping skills for dealing with each feeling that makes you vulnerable to relapse. Exactly what are you going to do when you have this feeling? Detail your specific plan of action. Some options are: Talk to my sponsor. Call a friend in the program. Go to a meeting. Call my counselor. Read some recovery material. Turn it over to my Higher Power. Get some exercise. For each feeling, develop a specific plan of action.

Feeling   _____
   Plan 1. _____
   Plan 2. _____
   Plan 3. _____

Feeling   _____
   Plan 1. _____
   Plan 2. _____
   Plan 3. _____

Interpersonal Conflict

Sixteen percent of people relapse when in a conflict with another person. They have a problem with someone, and they have no idea how to cope with the problem. The stress of the problem builds and leads to drinking or using drugs. This conflict usually happens with someone that you are closely involved with, wife, husband, children, parents, siblings, friends, or boss.

You can have a serious problem with anyone, even strangers, so you must have a plan for dealing with interpersonal conflict. You will develop specific skills in treatment that will help you communicate even when you are under stress.

You need to learn and practice the following interpersonal skills repeatedly.

1.   Tell the truth all the time.

2.   Share how you feel.

3.   Ask for what you want.

4.   Find some truth in what the other person is saying.

5.   Be willing to compromise.

If you can stay in the conflict and work it out, that's great, but if you can't, you have to leave the situation and get help. You may have to go for a walk, a run, or a drive. You might need to cool down. You must stop the conflict. You can't continue to try to deal with a situation that you feel is too much for you. Don't feel badly about this; interpersonal relationships are the hardest challenge we face. Carry a card with you that lists the people you can contact. You may want to call your sponsor, minister, counselor, fellow AA/NA member, friend, family member, doctor, or anyone else who may support you.

In an interpersonal conflict you will fear abandonment. You need to get accurate and reassure yourself that you have many people who still care about you. Remember that your Higher Power cares about you. God created you and loves you perfectly. Remember the other people in your life who love you. This is one of the main reasons for talking with others. When they listen to you, they give you the feeling that you are loved.

If you still feel afraid or angry, get with someone you trust and stay with that person until you feel safe. Do not struggle out there all by yourself! Every member of AA or NA will understand how you are feeling. We have all had these problems. We have all felt lost, helpless, hopeless, and angry.

Make an emergency card that includes all of the people you can call if you are having difficulty. Write their phone numbers down and carry this card with you at all times. Show this card to your counselor. Practice asking someone for help in treatment once each day. Write the situation down and show it to your counselor. Get into the habit of asking for help. When you get out of treatment, call someone every day just to stay in touch, and keep the lines of communication open. Get used to it. Don't wait to ask for help at the last minute, this makes asking more difficult.

Positive Feelings

Twelve percent of people relapse when they are feeling positive emotions. Think of all the times you used drugs and alcohol to celebrate. That has gotten to be such a habit, that when something good happens, you will immediately think about using. You need to be ready when you feel like a winner. This may be at a wedding, birth, promotion, or any event where you feel good. How are you going to celebrate without drugs and alcohol? Make a celebration plan. You may have to bring someone with you to a celebration, particularly in early recovery.

Positive feelings can also work when you are by yourself. A beautiful spring day can be enough to get you thinking about drinking or using. You need an action plan for when these thoughts pass through your mind. You must immediately get accurate and get real. In recovery we are committed to reality. Don't sit there and recall how wonderful you will feel if you get high—tell yourself the truth. Think about all the pain that chemical dependency has caused you. If you toy with positive feelings, you will ultimately use chemicals.

HOW TO SEE THROUGH THE FIRST USE

You need to look at how the illness part of yourself will try to convince you that you are not chemically dependent. The illness will flash on the screen of your consciousness all the good things that drugs and alcohol did for you. Make a list of these things. In the first column, marked Early Use, write down some of the good things you were getting out of using chemicals. Why were you using? What good came out of it? Did it make you feel social, smart, pretty, intelligent, brave, popular, desirable, relaxed, sexy? Did it help you sleep? Did it make you feel confident? Did it help you to forget your problems? Make a long list. These are the good things you were getting when you first started using. This is why you were using.

Early Use

1. _____
2. _____
3. _____
4. _____
5. _____
6. _____
7. _____
8. _____
9. _____
10. _____

Late Use

1. _____
2. _____
3. _____
4. _____
5. _____
6. _____
7. _____
8. _____
9. _____
10. _____

Now go back and place in the second column, marked Late Use. How you were doing in that area once you became chemically dependent? How were you doing in that same area right before you came into treatment? Did you still feel social or did you feel alone? Did you still feel intelligent or did you feel stupid? You will find that a great change has taken place. The very things that you were using for in early use, you get the opposite of in late use. If you were drinking for sleep, you couldn't sleep. If you were using to be more popular, you felt more isolated and alone. If you were using to feel brave, you were feeling more afraid. This is a major characteristic of chemical dependency.

Take a long look at both of these lists and think about how the illness is going to try to work inside of your thinking. The addicted part of yourself will present to you all of the good things you got in early use. This is how the disease will encourage you to use. But you must see through the first use to the consequences that are dead ahead.

Look at that second list. You must see the misery that is coming if you use chemicals. For most people who relapse, there are only a few days of controlled use before loss of control sets in. There are usually only a few hours or days before all the bad stuff begins to click back into place. Relapse is terrible. It is the most intense misery that you can imagine.

LAPSE AND RELAPSE

A *lapse* is the use of any mood-altering chemical. This is called a *slip*. A *relapse* is continuing to use the chemical until the full biological, psychological, and social disease is present. All of the complex biological, psychological, and social components of the disease become evident very quickly.

THE SLIP PLAN

You must have a plan in case you slip. It is foolish to think that you will never have a problem again. You must plan what you are going to do if you have problems. Hunt et al. (1971), in a study of recovering addicts, found that 33% of patients lapsed within 2 weeks of leaving treatment. Sixty percent lapsed within 3 months. At the end of 8 months, 63% had used. At the end of 12 months, 67% had used.

5.   I've had a hard day.

6.   My friends want me to drink.

7.   I never had a problem with pot.

8.   It's the only way I can sleep.

9.   I can do anything I want to.

10.   I'm lonely.

All of these inaccurate thoughts can be used to fuel the craving that leads to relapse. You must stop and challenge your thinking until you are thinking accurately. You must replace inaccurate thoughts with accurate ones. You are chemically dependent. If you drink or use drugs, you will die. That is the truth. Think through the first drink. Get honest with yourself.

HOW TO COPE WITH CRAVING

If you think inaccurately, you will begin craving. This is the powerful feeling that drives compulsive drug use. Craving is like an ocean wave—it will build and then wash over you. Craving doesn't last long if you move away from your drug of choice. If you move closer to the drug, the craving will increase until you are compelled to use. Immediately on feeling a desire to use, think this thought:

"That is no longer an option for me."

Now, drinking and using drugs are no longer an option. What are your options? You are in trouble. You are craving. What are you going to do to prevent relapse? You must move away from your drug of choice. Perhaps you need to call your sponsor, go to a meeting, turn it over to your Higher Power, call the AA/NA hotline, call the treatment center, call your counselor, go for a walk, run, visit someone. You must do something else other than thinking about chemicals. Don't sit there and ponder using—you will lose that debate. This illness is called the great debater. If you leave it unchecked, it will seduce you into using chemicals.

Remember, the illness must lie to work. You must uncover the lie as quickly as possible and get back to the truth. You must take the appropriate action necessary to maintain your sobriety.

DEVELOP A DAILY RELAPSE PREVENTION PROGRAM

If you work a daily program of recovery, your chances of success greatly increase. You need to evaluate your recovery daily and keep a log. This is your daily inventory.

1. Assess all relapse warning signs

    a. What symptoms did I see in myself today?

    b. What am I going to do about them?

2. Assess love of self.

    a. What did I do to love myself today?

    b. What am I going to do tomorrow?

3.   Assess love of others.

        a.   What did I do to love others today?

        b.   What am I going to do tomorrow?

An Intervention Plan For Resident Retention At The

Harbor Light Center

By

Eddie Olivas

PSN Manager

I.   Abstract: Resident Retention

The ongoing problem of client retention has been a challenge to most treatment Centers in the skid row for years. Due to the pervasive availability of crack cocaine, heroin, and alcohol many clients find it much more easier to walk down the street and acquire drugs, rather than stay in treatment. There is no doubt this community is mired by the illusion that drugs will be the elixir for the pain of isolation, addiction, societal racism, and the profound sense of personal failure. As we know, this is the deceptive nature of the disease of addiction. The problem of client recidivism is a significant problem because of what is at stake—lives and families. Today, even the threat of returning back to incarceration is not even a deterrent for most clients. In times past, the very mention of incarceration was enough to bring a client in a "space of compliance." Today, our population is most resistant or "treatment wise" and what worked yesterday may not work today. Hence, we have to innovate to address this pervasive problem regardless if the resident is a parolee or not.

II.   Purposed Intervention Plan For Resident Retention:

Throughout my varied background in the field of recovery, I have been fortunate to learn many different approaches that have dealt with the issue of Resident retention. This problem is clearly compounded by our location, population, and societal barriers that are consistent to this area. Hence, this problem is much more intensified for us.

My plan is rather simple, yet I believe it is the key to reducing this prevalent problem. The plan entails two primary changes in the way we conduct business on a daily basis, and it will require an organizational shift in the way we respond to this problem. Below are the changes that we would have to make to implement this plan with special emphasis on the Parolee population:

1. **Staff Intervention:** Once any staff member becomes aware of a client preparing to leave they are to alert key program managers and together they will perform an intervention. This intervention will allow the resident to receive different viewpoints on his/her decision to leave treatment. During regular business hours this protocol can be carried out with no real obstacles. On off hours (weekends) the plan would continue to be in effect; however, the intervention would be conducted with senior residents (bennies) and frontline staff. The primary aim is to support the resident during the contemplation of leaving treatment.

2. **Resident Contract/Mentoring Program:** The second aspect of this plan would entail an informal contract where the resident signs and promises that he/she will commit to at least 14 days of treatment, and if they need help they will ask for it. Also upon all admissions, a peer resident will be assigned to the resident to assist him/her in this critical time. Again the idea of a peer mentor and a contract is to support the resident and empower him/her to deal with the cravings, depression, and general discomfort of withdrawal.

III.   Conclusion:

In closing, the greatest resource we have in dealing with this population is you and I. Unfortunately, we do not have the means or the modality to deal with this problem like some other agencies simply because we are a social model detox; hence, we have to utilize our greatest resources, our expertise—you and I. This simply means key managers need to avail themselves to be more proactive with our residents. In short this plan is just the beginning effort in addressing this problem that many other providers in this area have come to accept as a fact of life

The state has halted construction of new dorms for the inmates at the California Rehabilitation Center in Norco while it considers whether to close the prison.

Norco prison may close by 2005

STATE COSTS: The decision will consider the center's drug-addiction recovery mission.

BY STEFANIE FRITH
THE PRESS-ENTERPRISE

NORCO—State fiscal problems, decline in the lower-security inmate population and a plan to release thousands of inmates from prison early could lead to the closure of the California Rehabilitation Center in Norco, officials said.

The California Department of Corrections is analyzing the Norco prison to see what it would take to close the institution by the year 2005, said corrections spokesman Russ Heimerich.

"CRC is the only institution we are looking at," Heimerich said.

Before making a decision, the state will consider the drug addiction recovery mission of the prison, as well as the more than $30 million spent on improvements in the last three years, Heimerich said. California Rehabilation Center offers the world's largest in-custody substance abuse program and is the only institution in the state to offer recovered inmates the chance to erase their felony convictions, said corrections Lt. Tim Shirlock of the Norco prison.

"The reason we are looking at this is because it's an older institution," Heimerich said. "There is a lot of . . . retrofitting that needs to be done that would cost a lot of money." The rehabilitation center was built in 1928 as the Lake Norconian Club, a luxury hotel. It later became a military hospital, and in 1962 was converted into the prison.

Last week, the state halted construction on the prison's $50 million dorm replacement project, which would have added 16 new dorms for the inmates. About $7 million has already been spent on the project,

PLEASE SEE PRISON, B2

Drug treatment program lets inmates look ahead

NORCO: If successful, their felony convictions for crimes committed while addicted will be erased.

BY STEFANIE FRITH
THE PRESS-ENTERPRISE

NORCO—Michelle Madewell, 26, has six children and is serving a six-year prison sentence for drug possession.

Leslie Simpson, 51, was addicted to cocaine and heroine. She says she'll do anything not to go back to her past. She was convicted of petty theft to pay for drugs.

Kelly Hecht, 44, wrote fraudulent checks to buy drugs. She said she comes from a dysfunctional family, but that doesn't excuse her actions.

Each of these women has a history of using drugs. And each of them was convicted of crimes they say they committed because of their drug addictions.

This is why they were sent to the California Rehabilitation Center in Norco. Sentenced as "civil addicts," they must complete a six-year program that includes a couple of years in prison, counseling once they are released and probation. If successful, their felony convictions will be erased from their records.

"All of us have the same issues: drugs, lack of a father, dysfunc-

tional family," Hecht said during a recent counseling session at the prison. "We learn here that we are not alone and that you gotta let go of the guilt and shame and get on with your life."

Only program in the state

There are about 1,200 male and female inmates at CRC who are part of the Civil Addict Program. The program is the only one in the state and was started in the early 1960s as part of a legislative effort to treat people who are uncooperative or unresponsive to treatment.

Last year, the prison began eliminating people from the program

PLEASE SEE **TREATMENT, B2**

VALERIE BERTA / THE PRESS-ENTERPRISE

Michelle Madewell, left, and Leslee White are participating in the Civil Addict Program at the California Rehabilitation Center in Norco.

205

TREATMENT

CONTINUED FROM B1

gram because of budget cuts to the California Department of Corrections, Warden Jo Ann Gordon said. No additional cuts were called for this year, but the program is still following through with cuts ordered last year.

The program has changed throughout the years as outside vendors like San Francisco-based Walden House contracted with the prison to work with drug-addicted convicts, Gordon said. Gordon pushed for more beds for civil addicts in the late 1990s, stating that for every dollar spent on treatment, the state saves $7. While inmates not in drug treatment programs have a return rate of about 64 percent, those in the Civil Addict Program have a return rate of about 18 percent, she said.

"I believe that in-custody treatment works," Gordon said. "But you have to marry it with aftercare. These people are going to be somebody's neighbor, and we need to help them become a successful member of society."

Some offenders ineligible

Not all drug offenders can be sentenced to CRC, Gordon said. A judge must feel that their crime was caused by their addiction to drugs. Sex offenders, arsonists and those who inflicted bodily harm during their crime will not be considered for the program, Civil Addict Program Capt. Riccardo Johnston said.

San Diego Superior Court Judge David Ryan, the county's first drug court judge, said he is a big proponent of sentencing people to CRC. People with substance abuse problems need to be treated, he said, otherwise they will continue to move around the criminal system.

"Many judges are opposed to rehabilitation because they want to seem tough on crime," Ryan said. "But we need to reduce the number of addicts. Illegal substance abuse by minors is growing, and there are at least 6 million hard-core users in the United States. Cocaine and heroine are more available than ever before."

Sending people to prison because they have drug issues may not be the answer, though, said San Bernardino Superior Court Judge John Martin. While he has sentenced people to CRC in the past, he would rather send someone to drug treatment programs through Prop. 36, an initiative that allows those convicted of drug crimes to attend programs instead of going to prison.

"I think there are more options available now than just sending someone to CRC," said Martin, who works in Redlands.

Drug treatment programs didn't work for Simpson, though. She spent time in prison and the House of Metamorphosis, a drug treatment center in San Diego.

"It wasn't until I came here that the light went on," said Simpson, who was convicted of petty theft with priors. "They really seem to listen here and give you feedback. I have a whole new outlook now."

Turning themselves in

Gordon agreed that drug treatment sometimes takes awhile to sink in. She said that when she was a parole officer in Northern California, parolees from CRC sometimes fell through the cracks and started taking drugs again. She would have to fly the parolees down to Norco and turn them back into the prison. Unlike any other state prison, civil addict parolees can walk up to the gate and turn themselves in for 60 days, she said.

"We've had mothers holding their sons by the ears and people be dropped off in taxis," she said. "It happens about four or five times a week. They are more than likely loaded when they get here, and they have to go cold turkey. It's tough to go back to prison. But they do it because they realize they need to help themselves."

Jennifer Klat, a 27-year-old mother from San Diego, said she didn't want to help herself when she was sentenced to CRC for child endangerment. She started taking prescription drugs and cocaine at age 20 and had been in and out of therapy for most of her life. It wasn't until she realized she was happy after therapy sessions that she realized she had to change.

"I started listening to the other women's stories, and I was so ashamed of myself," Klat said.

Mary Trautman, 38, of Yucca Valley said she was on "a bad road going nowhere fast" when she was sentenced for domestic violence after her teenager said she choked her. She said she was high on drugs at the time.

"I realized I had to work on me," Trautman said. "It's going to be a long process. But I'm working on it."

Reach Stefanie Frith at (909) 893-2114 or sfrith@pe.com

LOCAL

State move could shut prison

NORCO: Work is being halted on replacement dorms at the California Rehabilitation Center.

BY STEFANIE FRITH
THE PRESS-ENTERPRISE

The California Rehabilitation Center in Norco could be one of several state prisons to close as a result of a decision to release 15,000 lower-level prisoners by 2005, officials said Wednesday.

The prison population could decrease by from 6,000 to 15,000 by 2005 due to changes in the state budget that allow for some inmates to be paroled, prison wardens and officials were told Tuesday in a memorandum from California Department of Corrections Director Edward S. Alameida Jr.

"With the population reductions estimated at approximately 15,000 in the 2004/2005 fiscal year, it must be assumed that we may be facing prison/facility closures," Alameida wrote.

It has not been decided yet which, if any, prisons could close, said CDC spokesman Russ Heimerich. A team is being put in place this week to assess where cuts can be made.

"We are looking at the age of the institutions," said Heimerich. "It would make no sense to close down a newer institution or to leave an older institution."

He added that the state is trying to get prisons back to their designed capacities. Some prisons, such as the California Institution for Men in Chino, were designed for 2,778 inmates but now house 6,323, said Sgt. Arioma Sams. He noted that gyms and recreation rooms have been turned into dormitories to house the added inmates.

CRC in Norco is among the state's older prisons. It was built in 1928 as the Lake Norconian Club, a luxury hotel, and later became a prison.

Other older institutions include San Quentin State Prison, built in 1852, and Folsom State Prison, built in 1880.

PLEASE SEE PRISON, B6

STORY FROM B1

PRISON

CONTINUED FROM B1

Don Baumann, president of the California Correctional Peace Officers' Association for CRC, said the Norco prison sits very high on the cutting block. He said he has already been told that CRC will be closed and is now waiting for the official word, which will be turned into Alameida's office by Jan. 15.

He said it is unfair to consider closing the Norco facility because it has better retention rates of correctional officers than other prisons and does not have to spend as much on overtime pay for its officers. Overtime pay for correctional officers cost the state more than $255 million in 2002.

"We have a very good drug-treatment program here that would be difficult at best to duplicate at another prison," Baumann also noted.

Adding to speculation that CRC will close, construction on a $50 million dorm-replacement project at the prison could shut down as early as today. Sixteen dorms were scheduled to be built to replace 32 decrepit dorms built in the early 1940s. The first phase was scheduled to be finished in about a year. Heimerich said it "makes sense" to hold the line on some prison expenditures as the state figures out what to cut.

Many prison experts say California is doing the right thing by paroling inmates, but some say it's way past due, considering that many other states have been shutting down prisons and releasing inmates for years.

The state has 160,000 inmates in 32 prisons and about 112,000 parolees.

"The polls have shown that Californians want cuts made from prison spending," said Rose Braz, program director of Critical Resistance, an Oakland-based organization seeking to end the nation's dependence on prisons. "Other states are reducing their prison populations. California has not followed suit."

Corey Weinstein, a board member of the California Prison Focus, an inmate and family advocacy group in San Francisco, agreed, stating that a release of 15,000 inmates is too little and too long delayed. He said legislative analysts have talked for years about how the CDC can save money by releasing inmates who are older or near their parole dates. Unfortunately, he said, legislators see "being tough on crime" as a way to get elected.

"Some of these prisoners have served 15, 20 years," Weinstein said. "These are the kind of folks who tend not to violate their parole. They are very different people than when they came in."

Charles Skaags, Norco's interim city manager, said he understands the state's desire to parole inmates, but he hopes that it won't come to having to close CRC. Inmates from CRC clean up horse trails and do other work for the city, he said. There are also 1,500 employees at the prison.

"They are very worthwhile to have," Skaags said. "It would be a pretty good impact if it closed."

INMATE POPULATION

Total number of inmates in California's 32 state prisons:

160,000

Businesses ponder losing prison and bas[e]

NORCO: Businesses worry about losing the rehabilitation center and Naval Warfare Center.

BY PAIGE AUSTIN
THE PRESS-ENTERPRISE

NORCO—Many business owners, city officials and workers in Norco feel they're under economic siege with recent talk of closing down the prison and the Navy warfare center.

The California Rehabilitation Center and the Naval Surface Warfare Center pump hundreds of millions of dollars into the local economy. If they go, they'll take with them private corporations such as DynCorp, a technology company and Navy contractor with 300 local workers. Many fear that local restaurants, hotels and small businesses would struggle to survive.

The naval center barely escaped being shut down in 1995 during the Pentagon's last round of realignments and closures. Since then, community leaders have known the upcoming 2005 round of closures would be another fight for survival.

But when prison officials were told last week to halt construction of new dorms because of a possible closure, many were shocked.

The double-whammy would

JERRY SOIFER / THE PRESS-ENTERPRISE

The 6th Street Deli manager Sonya Guerico and Memo Velasquez work at the deli in Norco. It is one of the businesses that could be affected if the Naval Surface Warfare Center closes.

California Rehabilitation Center

Naval Surface Warfare Center Corona Division

COMMUNITY IMPACT

Naval Surface Warfare Center
Employees: 1,000
Annual payroll: $64 million

California Rehabilitation Center
Employees: 1,500
Operating budget: $77 million

THE PRESS-ENTER[PRISE]

The prison, the Navy and Corp employ nearly 2,500 p[eople] locally with salaries aver[age] between $45,000 and $7[...] The city receives state fu[nding] based on the size of its po[pula]tion, which includes the p[rison] population of about [...] inmates.

Norco relies on inmate [...] to help maintain its p[ublic] streets and trails. And c[ompa]nies such as DynCorp tha[t con]tract with the Navy are, in [...] required by the federal go[vern]ment to work with local businesses for goods and s[...]

have a crippling effect on Norco's economy, Mayor Harvey Sullivan said by phone.

"It will hurt the city big-time," he said.

PLEASE SEE CLOSU[RE]

Guards' heroism honored amid strife

CEREMONY: Nearly 200 Corrections employees are lauded with prison abuses as a backdrop.

BY DON THOMPSON
THE ASSOCIATED PRESS

SACRAMENTO—Correctional Officer Doug Drennan didn't make it to Friday's awards ceremony set against the backdrop of the state Capitol and a column of official color guards at parade rest.

He's still off work, recuperating from injuries he suffered during an inmate uprising in November at Calipatria State Prison. About 90 inmates overwhelmed guards there, seizing their batons and pepper spray canisters and turning them on the officers.

Correctional Officer Robert Moore stepped between a fallen guard and an inmate who was about to strike him with a baton. He along with Correctional Ser-

"Despite what you may hear and read about our department, our employees are dedicated individuals."

Director Jeanne Woodford

geants Basil Richards and Marin Morales and Correctional Officer Enrique Castillo were awarded gold star medals Friday, among nearly 200 Department of Corrections employees honored for heroism or service.

The event was a rare celebration for employees of the largest state prison system. For months they have endured steady criticism, including a series of state Senate hearings and a federal court-appointed monitor's finding that a system-wide "code of silence" protects wrongdoers while punishing whistleblowers.

"Despite what you may hear and read about our department, our employees are dedicated individuals," Director Jeanne Woodford told somber employees and joyful family members. "They represent professionalism and make me proud."

The 31,000-member California Correctional Peace Officers Association is so upset with Youth and Adult Correctional Secretary Rod Hickman that it distributed fliers this week accusing him of "leaving line officers and department personnel to twist in the wind" amid the criticism.

But Hickman, too, spent much of his day honoring those he called "truly some of California's most outstanding citizens."

Others awarded the department's second highest honor included two from Salinas Valley State Prison, which gained notoriety this year as home to a

band of rogue guards who called themselves "the Green Wall."

In this instance, Correctional Officers David Aldana and Vanessa Campos stepped in with batons and pepper spray as an inmate repeatedly stabbed a fellow guard in June while using him as a human shield against tower guards armed with rifles.

The guard required extensive stitches to repair wounds to his head, neck and hands, and prison officials credit Aldana and Campos with saving his life.

The final top award Friday went to Correctional Sergeant Michael L. Davis, who was driving a bus full of inmates along a narrow two-lane mountain road in September when the windshield was shattered by a piece of tire retread thrown up by a truck.

When Davis brought the 30-ton bus to a safe stop, he still had the tire retread draped across his chest.

Feds threaten takeover of state prisons

TROUBLED: A judge pans concessions in the guard deal, says receivership of the system is possible.

BY MARK GLADSTONE
KNIGHT RIDDER NEWSPAPERS

SACRAMENTO—Determined to reform the management of California's $6 billion-a-year prison system, a federal judge Tuesday threatened to take control of the Department of Corrections from the administration of Gov. Schwarzenegger.

In a letter to Schwarzenegger's top prison advisers, U.S. District Judge Thelton Henderson voiced disappointment that in recent contract renegotiations Schwarzenegger had agreed to concessions "that give up numerous and important management prerogatives" to the guards union.

The letter could jeopardize legislative approval of the renegotiated guard contract designed to save $108 million.

Henderson, who asked to meet with the governor, said recently negotiated contract provisions "subtly and some not so subtly" undermine the ability of the court to enforce orders, some of which are designed to improve the way the Department of Corrections investigates abuse of inmates and disciplines rogue officers.

"If the state of California is no longer willing to manage the necessary corrective actions, I must consider the appointment of a receiver," Henderson wrote in a letter Monday that arrived in the Capitol on Tuesday.

Peter Siggins, Schwarzenegger's legal affairs secretary, voiced "shock" and "disappointment" over Henderson's comments. He said the administration had met with the judge July 7 and expressed the governor's priority to reform prisons.

"I was probably the most surprised person on the planet this morning," Siggins said. He said Schwarzenegger would meet with Henderson but did not say when.

Siggins disputed the notion the administration had relinquished management controls to the union. Likewise, Lance Corcoran, executive vice president of the California Correctional Peace Officers Association, rejected suggestions that his union sought authority. Instead, he contended the union has pushed for improvements.

"We're frustrated with business as usual at the Department of Corrections as well," Corcoran said. "However, we're not an impediment to positive changes and never have been."

State Sen. Jackie Speier called the renegotiated contract a "policy swindle" and said receivership "may be the only thing that can right this ship." State Sen Gloria Romero said that the renegotiation was "weak" but said it was not a reason to launch a takeover.

THE PRESS-ENTERPRISE

DAVID
CORNWALL
PUBLISHER

MARIA
DeVARENNE
EDITOR

GALE
HAMMONS
**EDITORIAL PAGE
EDITOR**

PUBLISHERS OF
THE PRESS SINCE 1878
THE ENTERPRISE SINCE 1885
THE PRESS-ENTERPRISE SINCE 1932

HARRY HAMMOND
PRESIDENT 1937-1948

HOWARD H HAYS SR.
PRESIDENT 1948-1969

HOWARD H HAYS JR.
ARTHUR A. CULVER
**CO-PUBLISHERS
1965-1983**

HOWARD H HAYS JR.
PUBLISHER 1983-1988

WILLIAM D. RICH
PUBLISHER 1989-1993

MARCIA MCQUERN
PUBLISHER 1994-2002

OUR VIEW

Going 'girlie'

Sticks and stones may break my bones, but words will ... immobilize the state Legislature? How silly that Gov. Schwarzenegger's "girlie men" jibe has sent thin-skinned Democrats into a tailspin.

In response to the slam, indignant legislators vowed to stall the state budget for another two weeks. But talks with the administration resumed on Tuesday, with reported compromise on school-district contracting — one of the key hurdles to a final deal.

That said, humorless Democrats squandered precious days seething over a joke instead of doing their jobs.

Approving a budget is the Capitol's most vital responsibility. The deadline for the Legislature to fulfill its fiscal duties—

Schwarzenegger has shown a self-effacing sense of humor — oh yeah, and he's delivered a budget.

Schwarzenegger's point that the Democrats don't want to do their jobs.

Notwithstanding the feigned outrage from Sen. Sheila Kuehl, D-Santa Monica — The governor's homophobic! He's misogynist! — the "girlie man" reference had always been a jab at Schwarzenegger himself. A decade ago, Saturday Night Live's Dana Carvey and Kevin Nealon created the hysterical Hans and Franz to spoof the persona Schwarzenegger flaunted in his bodybuilding days.

June 15 — is enshrined in the state constitution. Yet more than a month has passed since that deadline, and Democratic leaders haven't allowed a vote on Schwarzenegger's May Revise ... or any other budget plan.

It's hard to figure why Senate and Assembly leaders insist on further delays, unless they're following the governor's script: They really are obstructionists who take directives from the public employee unions and other Capitol special interests. Any additional stalling by the Legislature only bolsters

By resurrecting that line to tweak Democrats, along with references from his own movies at other public events, Schwarzenegger has shown a self-effacing sense of humor, along with an eagerness to use pop culture to demystify the often mind-numbing job of governing.

Oh, and he's delivered a budget. It relies more on borrowing and gimmicks than we'd like, but it doesn't raise taxes. And it weight-lifts circles around the Democrats' alternative — which, to date, is nothing.

NEW YORK

GOP governors joining forces

The Republican governors of the nation's four most populous states announced Tuesday they were joining forces to lobby the federal government on issues of mutual interest.

"We represent over one-third of the nation's gross domestic product. Our states employ over 43 million people," the governors wrote to the leaders of Congress in a letter sent late last week.

The missive was signed by New York's George Pataki, the nation's longest-tenured governor; California's Arnold Schwarzenegger; Texas' Rick Perry; and Florida's Jeb Bush, brother of President Bush.

FROM NEWS SERVICES

THE PRESS-ENTERPRISE

DAVID CORNWALL
PUBLISHER

MARIA DeVARENNE
EDITOR

GALE HAMMONS
EDITORIAL PAGE EDITOR

PUBLISHERS OF
THE PRESS SINCE 1878
THE ENTERPRISE SINCE 1885
THE PRESS-ENTERPRISE SINCE 1932

HARRY HAMMOND
PRESIDENT 1937-1948

HOWARD H HAYS SR.
PRESIDENT 1948-1969

HOWARD H HAYS JR.
ARTHUR A. CULVER
CO-PUBLISHERS
1965-1983

HOWARD H HAYS JR.
PUBLISHER 1983-1988

WILLIAM D. RICH
PUBLISHER 1989-1993

MARCIA MCQUERN
PUBLISHER 1994-2002

OUR VIEW

A tough cell

Gov. Schwarzenegger wasn't exactly the antithesis of a "girlie man," to borrow his own lingo, in his recent talks with the state prison guards union.

In fact, his recent move to sweeten the guards' plush contract — yes, capitulation to a special interest — may cost more than the extra compensation. It may force the state to surrender control of the prison system.

U.S. District Judge Thelton Henderson said on Monday that this latest offer gave the guards' union too much sway over prison operations. Unless Schwarzenegger modified the deal, Henderson threatened to place a federal receiver in charge of state corrections.

Schwarzenegger should take the judge's admonition seriously, and solicit help from legislators who last month backed a more responsible deal with the guards. The governor should also revive the reform agenda he advanced in the early weeks of his administration.

After vowing to retool a Gray Davis sweetheart deal that called for an 11.3-percent pay hike this year, Schwarzenegger rewrote the pact in a way that made Davis look like a skinflint. Not only did Schwarzenegger endorse a 15 percent raise, he also vowed no layoffs, gave some guards leeway to set their own work assignments — no matter what their supervisors might prefer — and awarded union chapter presidents a day off each week, with pay, to work on union business.

Little wonder Henderson called this latest scheme "business as usual."

If Henderson appoints a receiver, the new boss would run the day-to-day operations of all 32 facilities. He or she could rewrite the guards' contract, setting compensation, workplace rules, even scheduling.

But the move would also strip state officials of any accountability for the prisons. A receiver could mandate new facilities, more guards or even higher compensation; the Legislature would then have to raise taxes or cut other public services.

Sen. Jackie Speier, D-Hillsborough, who's convened hearings on prison mismanagement, said the Legislature might reject the governor's latest deal, arguing the state can't afford it. She's right — and that move could force reasonable concessions from the union, while keeping the prison system in the hands of state officials, where it belongs.

THE PRESS-ENTERPRISE

DAVID
CORNWALL
PUBLISHER

PUBLISHERS OF
THE PRESS SINCE 1878
THE ENTERPRISE SINCE 1885
THE PRESS-ENTERPRISE SINCE 1932

MARIA
DE VARENNE
EDITOR

HARRY HAMMOND
PRESIDENT 1937-1948

HOWARD H HAYS JR.
PUBLISHER 1983-1988

HOWARD H HAYS SR.
PRESIDENT 1948-1969

WILLIAM D. RICH
PUBLISHER 1989-1993

GALE
HAMMONS
EDITORIAL PAGE
EDITOR

HOWARD H HAYS JR.
ARTHUR A. CULVER
CO-PUBLISHERS
1965-1983

MARCIA McQUERN
PUBLISHER 1994-2002

OUR VIEW

Guard the treasury

Legislators may be wising up, two years after Gray Davis mortgaged California's future in exchange for gobs of campaign money from the powerful prison guards' union.

Two-thirds of the Senate's Democrats, led by Jackie Speier of Hillsborough, pledged last week to block bloated pay hikes for prison guards.

Gov. Schwarzenegger's latest budget blueprint called for the cuts, which could trim the state deficit by $300 million.

It's about time. The platinum-plated contract handed the guards a 6.8 percent raise this year, with another 11.3 percent jump set to kick in July 1. As the state faces long-term deficits in the billions, such obscene pay hikes give budget-cutters a logical target.

And while Schwarzenegger says he'd rather retool Davis' contracts than watch the Legislature trim them piecemeal, the threat of legislative action could prod the guards and other unions to the bargaining table.

This carrot-and-stick approach from the governor and the Legislature could benefit all Californians, who deserve better than the sellouts and horse trades — state-financed perks for campaign cash — of the Davis years.

The union leadership's brazen role in this scheme has sullied the reputation of the hard-working guards on the front lines, who risk their lives daily to protect the law-abiding public from caged criminals.

Union officials have said that unless the Legislature retreats, the guards could take some form of "job action," although striking would be illegal. Any such move would be a mistake, both on the PR front and as a strategy to promote the interests of union members. Better to tone down the rhetoric, reopen negotiations with the governor and agree to a new contract more in line with common sense, private-sector standards and the fiscal imperatives of the state.

The platinum-plated contract handed the guards a 6.8 percent raise this year, with another 11.3 percent jump set to kick in July 1.

GUARDS: Contract under fire

CONTINUED FROM A1

but to come out swinging," Corcoran said.

The union quickly distributed fliers featuring Youth and Adult Correctional Secretary Rod Hickman on a milk carton: "Missing — last seen running for cover after promising to clean up the mess at CDC (California Department of Corrections), leaving line officers and department personnel to twist in the wind."

The flier offered a reward of "10,000 Rodney Bucks": 99-cent play money from "The Embarrassed State of California," bearing the slogan, "not worth a buck." Signatures on the fake money were those of Prison Law Office Director Don Specter, who has successfully sued over prison conditions and abuses, and state Sen. Jackie Speier, D-Daly City, who has chaired prison oversight hearings and organized the 17-senator voting bloc.

Even Speier, the most outspoken critic, is careful not to blame the union for doing what it has done so well.

"They've been very effective," she said. "They are a very persuasive organization. I don't fault them, I fault the administration that negotiated the contract for doing a lousy job."

The union has weathered prison scandals before, but is suddenly vulnerable because of a confluence of circumstances.

"To be honest, they look a little like crybabies. I don't think they're going to get a lot of public sentiment," said UC Berkeley political scientist Bruce Cain.

The union helped elect both Republican Gov. Pete Wilson and Democrat Davis with singularly large campaign contributions. But new Republican Gov. Arnold Schwarzenegger refused to take the union's money. He now wants the union to give back $300 million from its contract, the bulk of the $465 million he's seeking from all unions to help trim the budget deficit.

"The CCPOA contract was standing out like a sore thumb when everybody else was cutting back," Cain said. More than simply generous, the Davis-negotiated contract included concessions that concerned even union-backing Democrats.

Attorney General Bill Lockyer is challenging one provision requiring investigators to turn over confidential information to prison employees who are under investigation. State Sen. Gloria Romero, D-Los Angeles, a union stalwart who declined to sign the 17-member contract pact, won unanimous Senate support for her bill blocking the clause.

Romero has chaired a series of critical Senate hearings into a series of scathing reports by national experts into conditions at the California Youth Authority, and into what a federal court-appointed watchdog said is a systemwide "code of silence" that protects wrongdoers while punishing whistleblowers. Critics say the only thing preventing a federal takeover of the system is Schwarzenegger's promises of reform.

The second unanimously approved bill last week would substitute a new code of conduct for that code of silence.

State lawmakers turn tables on

SHOWDOWN: The labor group faces challenges to its contract and a new drive for jail reform.

BY DON THOMPSON
THE ASSOCIATED PRESS

SACRAMENTO—Over the past quarter-century, California's prison guards union grew into perhaps the most feared force in state politics, as it used its money, connections and go-for-the-jugular instincts to reward its friends and, more importantly, punish its enemies.

That may have changed last week.

Twice in three days, senators voted unanimously against the California Correctional Peace Officers Association, reversing years of a symbiotic relationship in which lawmakers voted in near lockstep with the union in return for financial and political support.

And on the third day, 17 Democratic senators, two-thirds of the caucus that controls that chamber, vowed to undo what may be the union's crowning achievement: a fi year contract fattened by ca paign contributions to form Gov. Gray Davis and project to deliver cumulative 37 perce pay raises to the union's 31,0 members.

"As public officials, we ca not operate under threats. can't operate with threats th have to do with labor unrest, v

prison guards union

can't operate under threats that have to do with lower incomes that we might receive, or contributions. We have to do what we believe is in the best interest of the public," said state Sen. Jack Scott, D-Altadena, one of the 17.

Union Executive Vice President Lance Corcoran warned of "a long, hot summer" of potential prison unrest by disgruntled guards. The union already has doubled the half-million dollars it usually spends each year for public relations, with the extra $500,000 going toward a half-minute television ad and half-hour documentary on prison conditions.

"All it's done is to back us into a corner, and we have no choice

PLEASE SEE GUARDS, A7

About The Author

Dan O'Farrell is the on-site coordinator and Education Counselor for the LA County Parole Services Network at the California Rehabilitation Center in Norco, California. CRC is a 5000 ± inmate prison housing both men and women.

Mr. O'Farrell holds a BA Degree from California State University at Fullerton and Credentials in Alcohol and Drug Studies. Victimology and Human Services from Cypress College in Cypress, California.

www.ingramcontent.com/pod-product-compliance
Lightning Source LLC
Chambersburg PA
CBHW080409290526
45791CB00008BA/2205